Get Over Your Damn Self

The No-BS Blueprint to building a Life-Changing Business

ROMI NEUSTADT

Published by:
LiveFullOut Media
www.LiveFullOut.com

A portion of the profits of every book supports charities that empower the health and education of women and children.

ISBN: 978-0-9979482-1-9

Library of Congress Control Number: 2016950761

For Nate and Bebe: Thank you for giving me the hardest and most rewarding profession on the planet and for being my best teachers. May you always share your gifts and your light so you LiveFullOut and make the world a better place.

For John: Love of My Life, thank you for helping me become the woman I always wanted to be. And for loving all of me. Even the not-so-great parts.

For you, the Reader: Thank you for daring to design the life you really want. Your guts and grit will not only allow you to step into your greatness, but will also inspire others to do it too. And thank you for believing you're worth it, because you are.

For Me: Thank you for not giving up on your lifelong dream of writing a book. For having the balls to really put yourself out there in the hopes that it helps some people. And for telling the negative voices in your head to shut the hell up. Yes, you ate an entire bag of popcorn last night and forgot to send the kids to school with their field trip forms this morning. But you wrote a friggin' book! #winning

CONTENTS

Let's Get This Party Started

If I had my way, you and I would get to have a weekly coffee date so I could tell you all I've learned over the last six years. We'd get to know each other; we'd talk about our husbands, our kids, our challenges and fears. We'd talk about our businesses and our lives. It's my favorite part of this gig. I'd learn about you and you'd learn about me. We'd get to help each other grow, not just as business owners, but as women.

Unfortunately, that's just not possible. When I started out in this business, I loved being able to touch every new person on our team—whether in person or virtually. But as my team started to grow into what are now tens of thousands of business partners in multiple countries, I haven't been able to touch or mentor all of our team members, let alone all the people who've reached out to me from around our company and the profession.

This book is the next best thing to us being able to get together. I've reviewed all that I've learned and all of my experiences—good and bad—and put it all together to help you learn how to talk your way to the life you really want.

First, let's talk about you. You may have just started your business a few weeks or months ago, or you perhaps you've been around the profession longer. Either way, the minute you opened this book, you started a new level of commitment, focus, fun (I hope), and personal and professional growth.

Maybe you're a working mom who's trying to build an exit strategy from a job that has you juggling work and kids, and you feel like you're failing miserably. Perhaps you used to be a professional powerhouse who set aside your career because you couldn't figure out how to be a working hands-on mom. But now you're ready to have an identity outside of mom and wife, and to make your own money. Or maybe you're just a super-savvy woman who understands how brilliant it is to develop another stream of income that can grow while you sleep. No matter what your background or your reason why you're a part of our profession, I think you'll get a lot out of our time together. I've helped thousands of women just like you build everything from travel and college funds, to replacement incomes that allowed them and/or their husbands to retire from their day jobs, to finally having the freedom and security they didn't even think was possible. Now I'm going to help you get to where you want to be!

I wrote this book to help you create the kind of business your team will want to emulate, and the duplication that you need to create to get you where you want to go, not just in this profession, but in life. I hope that throughout these pages, you'll experience a powerful increase in your confidence and a greater understanding of how to be the leader you want on your team. Everyone has the potential to grow the business of their dreams. And you do too. You *can* be a successful CEO of your business, while creating and living the life you really want.

I'm going to teach you the skills and strategies you need to build a lucrative network marketing business. Or direct sales business. Or social marketing business. Or community commerce business. But whatever you want to call this profession you're now a part of, we'll work on your understanding of the basics and how to do the necessary income-producing activities better and more efficiently. But if that's all there was to this biz, there would be a hell of a lot more seven-figure success stories.

It takes more than skills to advance in title and grow a large organization. It also requires an understanding and awareness of the mindset and behaviors you need to reach your big goals. This business is built between the ears, so I'm gonna mess with your head a bit.

Building a successful network marketing business isn't just about developing your business. It's about developing you. Ask any of the top leaders around the profession and they'll tell you that this inner work is even more important to get to the big bucks and time freedom.

I'm not going to spend a lot of time talking about social media because entire books can and have been written about that. I also don't cover events since I trust your company and your upline have a successful way to execute events that are specific to your company and your products. What I do share with you is everything I know about having the most authentic and effective conversations with people, those you know and those you meet. And how to reframe the most important conversations you'll ever have—the ones you have with yourself.

Since you're going to let me mess with your head, you should know a little about me. I'm probably not a lot different than you. I'm a mom of two beautiful kids, Nate and Bebe, and wife to the love of my life, John. I was a corporate chick—first a lawyer (which I completely hated), then an award-winning public relations executive in both New York and Seattle. I married a doctor (my Jewish mother was very proud), and John had a thriving practice.

Despite being a two-professional household, we were getting by, but not getting ahead. College and retirement funds weren't getting filled, we didn't have the time freedom to put our kids first, and we were both tied to the fee-for-service model. We were at the beck and call of our clients and patients, and if we didn't work, we didn't get paid.

After 12 years of doing just about every type of PR work out there, I was bored out of my mind. I wanted a new adventure. I wanted to stop hitting my head against an earnings glass ceiling. I wanted a richer life—sure, more money, but also complete time flexibility for my family and for me, and the ability to have a positive impact on others.

It's pretty amazing what the universe brings you when you ask for it. I learned about my company from a new PR client of mine at the time. I immediately fell in love with the idea of joining an established global brand that had moved into direct sales and being able to build a business of my very own without having to build an infrastructure. John and I both agreed I had to do this.

When I started, I had an insanely full plate. Nate was three, Bebe was six months old, I had a thriving PR consultancy and had taken on way too many clients, I was sitting on non-profit boards, teaching Hebrew school, helping John out with aspects of his medical practice and his dietary supplement start-up, I was routinely helping my elderly mom, and I was trying to lose baby weight. But because I simply couldn't pass this up, I decided to get a bigger plate!

I was coachable and consistent and added at least three to five new business partners and a handful of customers every month. In my first year I was named my company's Top Recruiter and had built a six-figure income. Less than two-and-a-half years into my business, John was able to walk away from his clinical practice, focus all his professional efforts on his start-up, and be more of a hands-on dad. In less than three years, less time than it took me to get through law school, I had earned a million dollars.

Four years in, John's supplement company was requiring little of his time, and he considered going back into clinical practice. Luckily for me and our team, he ultimately decided that he could have the greatest impact on people by working alongside me. So he jumped in too.

Now, with a six-figure monthly income, we earn much more than we could in medicine or Corporate America. But more valuable than the money is the ability to have complete flexibility over all aspects of our lives, putting Nate and Bebe first, and allowing us to pay our success forward in causes dear to our hearts. We've both fallen in love with this business model. To be successful, it requires that we help others succeed and help them build the businesses and lives of their dreams. Through this gift of a profession, we've found renewed purpose and a deep sense of professional satisfaction.

John and I are most proud of our tens of thousands of team members who dare to believe that it's possible to have their cake and eat it too. These fun, visionary dreamers have become like family, and we can't imagine life without them or this profession. I've included some of their stories in this book because there's much to learn from them.

So more than six years into this adventure, I knew it was time to share what I've learned. Because I'm a no-BS kind of girl, I'm not going to sugar coat a thing. This is a business, and if you're serious about learning exactly what it takes to build it big, you've come to the right place. But I'm going to ask you to get, as one of the top leaders on our team Linda Lackey Ray says, "real and raw." You have to be willing to be honest with yourself and do the things I'm going to ask you to do. If you're brave enough, I promise it will be worth it.

Speaking of brave enough, although I have a journalism degree and have written a lot in my career, this is my first book. Honestly, writing it scared the shit out of me. But, as I'm going to teach you (and I promise to never ask you to do something I'm not willing to do), life begins at the edge of, and keeps expanding outside of, our comfort zone. So here goes.

I hope you realize how insanely lucky you are to be in this profession. Those of us in network marketing get to decide what our lives look like, and to help other people do the same. Travel, time with our kids, getting involved in causes near and dear to our hearts—you're sitting on a business that can give you all of that.

When I was standing in your shoes, I didn't quite understand where this was going to take me or my family. But I am living proof that a six-figure monthly income is possible, and that it's possible for you too. That making enough money to allow your spouse to pursue exactly what he wants is possible. That designing your life around your kids is possible. And traveling to your bucket list is possible. Volunteering your time to causes and donating more money that you used to earn is possible. If you're not thinking that big, if you're not thinking about limitless possibilities, it's time for you to start. And I'm going to help you get there.

Let's go!

XO,

CHAPTER 1

Why People Fail and Why That Ain't Gonna Be You

Congratulations, you are the CEO of your own business! Granted, none of us need to do much of the heavy lifting that CEOs of traditional businesses must do. We don't have to build an infrastructure, source raw materials or manufacturers. We don't have to figure out our distribution channel or build out a technology platform or hire a marketing team or an HR department or any of the other gazillion things that go into building a traditional product or service company from the ground up. All we have to do is talk to people—share our love of our products and our company.

If it's that easy, you may be asking why the heck you need this book. And why aren't more people in our profession six- and seven-figure earners?

Wait a minute; I didn't say anything about "easy." This biz is anything but EASY. It's hard. Really hard. It's going to test you in ways you never imagined. It will have tremendous highs and cavernous lows. It will require you to dig deep and learn resilience—to get so clear on who you are and what you stand for. It will be a roller coaster that will sometimes have you thinking that you're going to fly off, and other times it will make you want to hurl.

I told you I'm a no-BS kinda girl. If you want a sugar-coated version of this biz, then you've come to the wrong place. The reality is that this business will test you, just like every other worthwhile goal will. Want to run an Ironman? You better be prepared to train, and train, and train some more. And sweat. A lot. Want to raise well-adjusted, happy children? You better be prepared to be tested over and over, and be willing to learn about your own shortcomings, and be willing to stretch and grow (and get some serious gray hairs). Want to grow a six- or seven-figure business? You really want to get there? Then you better be willing to dig in, stretch yourself and work through good times and bad.

No. This business isn't easy. But it is simple. Laughably simple. We share about our business and our products. And the people we talk to fit into three buckets.

The Three Buckets

The first bucket contains the people who want to become our customers. They order and fall in love with our products or services and keep reordering from us. They become walking, talking billboards and refer us business.

Then there are others who see what we see from a business perspective and they join our teams. They fit into the second bucket. It may include people who get it right away and jump in. Or it might be happy product customers, when it finally dawns on them—even though we've already told them—that instead of referring people to someone else they could actually be creating another stream of income for themselves and their families. So they convert to business builders and join our team. Anyone who comes on board learns this simplistic, duplicable system. We teach them to do exactly what we do—talk to people and add customers and team members.

There are others who aren't interested in our products or services or our businesses, and they fall into the third bucket. We ask them to connect us with people in their networks who just might be a great fit. They become referral sources.

We keep doing this day after day, month after month, and after a few years of consistently showing up and doing the work, we have a thriving business that can do everything from fill vacation, college and retirement funds to provide career exit strategies and build transformative wealth.

That's our business. That's it. It only took four short paragraphs to spell it out. That's how simple it is. But again, you may be asking, if it's that simple, why the heck aren't there more six- and seven-figure earners in our profession? THAT'S the million-dollar question and the one we'll answer in this book to help you unlock your greatest potential and create the business and the life you dream of.

The Four Reasons Why People Fail

After six years in this gig, I've learned the four reasons why people fail.

Reason #1: They're not coachable.

We've already established that this is a simple system, laughably so. It's not rocket science and anyone—regardless of background, or professional or educational pedigree—can learn how to do it. But it requires us to be open to learning this simple system. If someone isn't seeing success, it's almost always because they're not following the system, either because they don't trust it or because they're arrogant enough to think they can do it faster, stronger, better.

I came to this profession with a law degree, a brief-but-successful stint as a lawyer, and an award-winning PR career. One could argue that I had professional chops and knew how to make shiz happen. But like so many who come to network marketing, I had zero experience in this gig, and knew I had to do everything possible to learn. I did what the successful members of my upline told me to do—I plugged into the resources of my company and I became a student of the profession. I did exactly what I was coached to do. Once I learned the basics, I was able to add my own personality, flair and experience to the mix, but not until I knew what the hell I was doing.

Would I have walked into a deposition to interview a potential witness without first learning the procedure? Would I have written my first press release without first learning what needs to go into the release and how to construct it? Admittedly, my tenth deposition was a hell of a lot better than my first, and after three months of writing releases, I could practically do it in my sleep. But at the beginning I learned the SYSTEM. And this business is no different.

> **Make a commitment to be 100% coachable. Declare it right now.**

Whether you're brand new to our profession or you've been plugging away for a while and your business isn't where you hoped it would be, make a commitment to be 100% coachable.

Get in Action

Declare it right now wherever you are, even if you're on an airplane, in the chair at the salon with a bunch of foils on your head, or next to your sleeping hubby: "I am 100% coachable!"

Did you do it? Did you declare, "I am 100% coachable?" If you did, then you've already sailed over your first success hurdle. You passed the first test.

If you didn't declare it—and I don't want you to say it unless you really, completely believe it—then don't read any further.

Stop. Set this book down or better yet give it to someone who wants help. Someone who's willing to be 100% coachable.

Why is this coachable piece so important? If you're not coachable, you won't talk to enough people. I've seen this over and over, too many times to count, so I know this to be an indisputable fact. It's as true as saying that your next bikini wax is going to hurt like hell. When I say you have to talk to people ALL THE DAMN TIME, I am not kidding!

The *uncoachables*, as we like to call them, also refuse to implement proven business building tools to help them expose and close—expose their network to what they're offering and move them through their funnel to a close. So if you're one of the uncoachables, again, please put this book down. It's not for you.

But if you are coachable, keep reading. Being coachable is the first step, but that's only part of the story. It doesn't end when you learn the basics. Becoming a professional network marketer, turn-key entrepreneur, social marketer, direct sales professional, or whatever you want to call yourself, requires you to become a student of the profession. To embark on a never-ending quest to learn how to do what we do better. So buckle up Buttercup, because this is a long, winding, wonderfully exciting ride of constant learning, growth and evolution.

Reason #2: They don't treat this like a business.

You've likely heard this tried and true fact: If you treat your business like a hobby, it will pay you like a hobby. But if you treat it like a real business, it can pay you like a business. I don't think people actually believe this is a get-rich-quick scheme, or that it's going to fall from the sky into their laps. I just think that too many people start their businesses thinking that this out-of-the-box business model doesn't require the

> To turn your venture into a successful business, you must make it a priority and carry your business with you wherever you go.

same consistency and commitment that other businesses do.

Give me an example of a CEO who has built a successful six- or seven-figure company who didn't consistently show up to build it, and I'll send you a personal gift from me. Or show me an example of a person who got a job and only showed up when they felt like it and didn't get fired. Let's get real, it's called net**work** marketing not net**slacker** marketing!

The beautiful thing is, in our profession, you don't have to devote 40 or 50+ hours a week every single week to see big gains. But those part-time hours of income-producing activities (IPAs) that we coach you to put in every week? We really mean you need to do them EVERY week. Even when you're tired, deflated, disappointed, frustrated, and ready to pull your hair out.

To turn your venture into a successful business, you must make it a priority and carry your business with you wherever you go. If you owned a retail store instead of a virtual business, you'd go to the brick-and-mortar space and turn around the "Open" sign and get to work. How can you expect to be open for business if you're not turning around the "Open" sign in your brain and in your schedule? In this profession, every time your mouth is closed your business is closed.

In these pages we'll talk a lot about how to spend your time. You should devote at least 80% of your time to your personal business: talking to people, finding those who want to be your customers and giving them the best possible service, finding those who want to join your team and training these newbies (those in the first 30 days of their business). We call this paying yourself first in order to keep growing. Ten percent should be devoted to three-way calls for your team (I can't wait to teach you about the most powerful closing tool we've got), and 10% should be spent on your personal training (plugging into training calls or webinars , attending in-person training events) and the coaching of your non-newbie business partners.

For example, if you're devoting 15 hours a week to your business, at least 12 hours will go to your personal business (prospecting and training your newbies), 1.5 hours will go to three-ways, and 1.5 hours will go to your personal training and coaching your non-newbies. You may be gasping here about spending so little on coaching others, but you'll learn later why this time allocation formula is so important to keep you growing, and to help you avoid putting the brakes on or even crashing your business.

Since our business can be blissfully flexible around life happening, we're able to maneuver around those hours as needed. But they must happen! If you miss your hour in the morning to smile and dial because your babysitter is sick, the dog just pooped on the carpet, and you've got to deal with a broken washer, that's ok. Just make up the hour later in the day or the next day.

> This business requires you to get comfortable being uncomfortable.

Speaking of babysitters, it always makes me giggle when a stay-at-home mom of little ones who aren't in school yet thinks she can build a six- or seven-figure business solely around her kids' hour-long nap time each day. Yes, that hour can be wildly productive and you should definitely capitalize on it. As we'll discuss later in this book, it's so much fun to make connections and fill your funnel while doing things with your kids in the normal course of your day. But it's unrealistic to think you won't need more uninterrupted time, so investing in a babysitter a few hours a week can make an exponential difference in your long-term success. Remember, you're the CEO of your own business. Tell me about a mom of littles who became a successful CEO—of a start-up no less—who didn't have at least a few hours a week of childcare so she could focus on her biz uninterrupted. If you come up with one, email me at info@livefullout.com and I'll send you a prize, and I'll eat crow.

Reason #3: They're not willing to get uncomfortable.

This business requires you to get comfortable being uncomfortable, at least in the beginning. Most of us have never done this type of business so we can feel awkward and vulnerable. Too often, new business builders hide behind getting ready to get ready, because it's safer. I've seen a slew of team members who never gave themselves the opportunity to fly because they wouldn't take off. They busy themselves with assembling binders of information, setting up a home office, color-coding a filing system, and writing and rewriting their list of people.

They keep practicing talking to people instead of actually talking to people, assuming they're supposed to sound like established leaders. This isn't the type of endeavor where you study and study and then apply what you've learned. It only works if you allow yourself to earn as you learn, relying on the system and the people who've come before you. We all have to muck our way through those first few months before we start to get the hang of it.

Then after a bit of success, followed by a hiccup or two, it's common to see business builders go into management mode with the team they have instead of continuing to put themselves out there and keep building. But your business won't continue to grow if you don't keep putting yourself out there over and over again. That means you're going to fall and make mistakes. But I know from experience, you'll only grow really big if you're willing to make mistakes and then learn from them. As I tell our kids, if you're not making mistakes, you're not stretching yourself and you're not trying hard enough.

Reason #4: They're not hungry enough.

This is the biggie, and it's epidemic in our business. I've had loads of business partners who have access to kickass training, not just from me, but from exceptional leaders around our team and the rest of our company. They're coachable and willing to learn how to do this. They're even consistent...for a while. But then something happens. That thing called life. It gets in the way. The kids get sick, there's a big project at their day job. They're tired. There's a really good episode of Scandal on. So their business gets moved way down on their list of priorities.

Life happens to all of us every single day. We're all working with the same 24 hours. So why do some people stop working their businesses because life happens, while others of us keep working our businesses in spite of everything life throws at us?

Because we're hungry. I mean really hungry. Think I-haven't-had-a-carb-in-six-months kind of hungry.

I was starving. Not literally, but I wasn't living the life I wanted for me or my husband or our kids. Suddenly, that reality was sitting like a ton of bricks on my shoulders. I couldn't find a way out of the billable hour jail and the daily grind that was boring me into a numbed version of myself.

I looked down the road five and ten years into the future and was scared to death. I saw a future of getting by, but not getting ahead. Not giving our kids all the things I wanted

> **I was willing to do whatever it took to build it. This had to work.**

for them, let alone all the things John and I had dreamed of and talked about when we were dating before we had our kids. So when this profession landed in my lap, I just knew this was our way out of a ho-hum life.

I was willing to do whatever it took to build it. This had to work. Even when I was juggling our baby, our toddler, my PR clients, volunteering, doing work for John's biz, helping my aging mom, and trying to lose baby weight, I was juggling, and inelegantly at that. I was tired and scared and often disappointed and deflated. But there were little and big victories that gave me small glimpses of what this could really be.

So I kept going. Even before we were making big money, I saw this succeeding. I visualized the taste of freedom that would come with bigger commissions and residual income and the ability to stop working for others. I could taste the amazing freedom my husband would experience when he could walk away from a clinical practice he no longer loved to pursue work that would feed his soul. I could see our family frolicking on family vacations at luxury resorts, and I could taste the sweetness of getting to live life on our terms. I wanted this so badly that nothing, and I mean nothing, was going to stop me.

It was the same for my friend and business partner, Tracy Willard. Her family was hungry, literally. The Great Recession caused her husband's exciting new start-up to go south, leaving her family to get by on her low-paying job teaching at the local university. With bills mounting and more month than money, Tracy had to go to the food bank to feed her girls. They were forced to sell their home in a short sale to avoid foreclosure, and they moved in with her in-laws. Completely broke, she had to get a loan from her parents to start her business.

When she joined our team, she was so desperate to get up from rock bottom that she was 100% coachable, consistent, and kept putting one foot in front of the other, no matter the obstacles. She was volunteering every spare minute so that her girls could participate in activities for free (because they couldn't afford to pay for them), and teaching, and trying to keep her family together (and I mean that literally—not just to keep her family afloat, but struggling to keep her family physically together). Despite this, Tracy was profitable in her first full month. In less than two years, she went from food stamps to earning a free Lexus courtesy of our company. Her hunger fueled her commitment and consistency, and today Tracy and her beautiful family are living their dreams in a house by the beach in Southern California.

Please understand, I'm not suggesting that you can't be successful in this business unless you're at your wit's end with your life or unable to feed your family. But you've got to figure out *what it is that you really want* that you don't already have. Whatever it is, it's got to be important enough to get you to do something with commitment and consistency. It's got to be important enough to get you up, to make one more phone call, to reach out to one more person, and to loop back with one more prospect—even when you're bone-ass weary. Because if we want something bad enough in this life, we make it happen. It's just that simple.

Now that we've gotten that out of the way...

So now we're clear on why people don't succeed. Maybe I've even described you up till now. But what if you dig deep and start to dream bigger so that your hunger propels you into action that not only changes life for you and your family, but also inspires others to change their lives too?

> What if you dig deep and start to dream bigger so that your hunger propels you into action?

What if you could learn how to do the system better so that you were more comfortable talking to people about your business and your products?

What if you could learn how to think like the CEO of a six- or seven-figure business and make decisions about your time and your team through that filter?

I can't make you coachable and I can't motivate you. That has to come from you. But in the following pages, I can coach you through all the other stuff. So let's put on our big girl panties, dig real deep, and let me help you grow something that you'll not only be proud of, but that could end up changing your life!

If that sounds good, let's really get this party started.

CHAPTER 2

Why Are You Here?

If you've been in this profession for any time at all, somewhere in your training, you've been asked to figure out your reason WHY for wanting to build a business. Some say your WHY has to be big enough to make you cry. Well, I don't know about the crying part, but it's definitely got to be big enough to keep you consistently showing up for your business, week after week, month after month.

There are so many things in life vying for your time and attention that if you don't really want to do this, you won't. It will never be a priority and you'll stay stuck in an endless, vicious cycle: you're not working on your business because it's not tied to something you really want; you're beating yourself up because you're not working on your business; you're not working your business because it's now all about guilt and failure because you're beating yourself up for not working on your business. That's neither fun nor lucrative. In fact, it makes me exhausted just writing about it.

Do you know WHY you want to build a business of your own? I've had so many conversations with team members over the last five years who complain that they just can't seem to stay committed to their businesses and routinely do the income-producing activities required to see results. The vast majority of the time, when I ask them WHY they're building their business, they answer with some variation of "I'm not sure." If you can't see it, smell it, taste it. If it doesn't move you deep in your soul,

> If you can't see it, smell it, taste it. If it doesn't move you deep in your soul, then I promise you, it's not enough to keep you committed.

then I promise you, it's not enough to keep you committed.

When you figure out your WHY, you've got to share it with your business partner and the rest of your support team (your spouse, BFF, other family members). They've got to know what it is so that they can keep you accountable when it gets hard to keep your eyes on the prize.

I'm a big believer that your WHY can't be about money, but it can be about *what the money will do for you.* And it has to be deeply personal to you. I've worked with a lot of people who have made their WHY about other people. Maybe it was their kids or their husband. I'm here to tell you right now, that in order to get yourself way out of your comfort zone during the scary, uncomfortable start of your business, your WHY has to be about **you**.

I was doing training for a portion of our team, and I went around the room asking the women what their WHY was. When I got to someone whom I'll call Maria, she said it was to pay for her kids' college. Yet there was no fire in her eyes when she said it, just a soft voice coming out of a dipped head and slumped shoulders. I respectfully challenged her, "You started your business over a year ago and still aren't showing up consistently to work it. Could it be that your reason WHY isn't enough to get you to do this?"

"But of course it should be, it's my children," she argued.

"Aha," I said, "you think it should be, but it's not." Then I asked her to tell me what she really wanted for herself. As her eyes welled up with tears, she admitted that she really wanted to have something of her very own outside of mom and wife, and to prove to herself that she could accomplish big things.

As she said it, something incredible happened—her voice got stronger, her shoulders moved up and back, and she sat taller.

"That's your real WHY, my dear," I said to her as I hugged her. "That's what will get you to do this every damn day." Since then, Maria has engaged in her business with a consistent determination that wasn't there before. She's moved past the level she'd been stuck at and has reached a major promotion and pay raise.

> You need a bulletproof WHY to get you through the tough times. And that WHY has to be about you and for you.

We women are programmed to do everything for others. But I promise you, building this business for others won't be enough. You need a bulletproof WHY to get you through the tough times. And that WHY has to be *about you* and *for you.*

Being part of something new and fun, filling up your time while the kids are at school, or quelling your fear of missing out on something—while these might be reasons enough to get you to jump in and reach a certain level of success, they're not nearly enough to keep you doing the heavy lifting that is required to build a six- or seven-figure business.

I added on a personal business partner, Pamela Mulroy, after she watched me for months on Facebook and then saw our company's products on the Today Show. At the time, she loved the idea of doing something new and liked the idea of transitioning out of her part-time career. That was enough to get her to the first substantial title in our company and to step away from her day job. But once that goal was met, Pamela didn't have a reason to keep building. Without continued recruiting, she demoted in title. For a couple years, I was unable to extract a reason why she wanted to build this business. But without it she had no reason to work enough to recapture her title and collect the significant money she left on the table every month, let alone go after the free Lexus that's within her reach.

It is possible, however, to have a breakthrough if you can discover a new, more powerful WHY. Pamela decided she wanted to take a lot of the financial pressure off of her hard-working husband Tom, and this new goal ignited a new commitment and dedication to her business. And Pamela's certainly not the only one.

Becca O'Leary first started her business to have some "adult interaction and something apart from being a mommy." But after two years of slow growth, she had an epiphany while attending a training event put on by our company. She had been dragged to the event by her sponsor and best friend. Sitting there listening to the success stories, she discovered a new WHY. "I finally got it. I felt so guilty that my husband was carrying all the financial stress for our family. I didn't want to live with guilt. I wanted to feel like I was contributing and playing a role in supporting our family. That's when I made the decision to treat this like a business." It's a WHY that was big enough for Becca to start running all the way to the top of the pay plan.

My dear friend Amy Hofer first started her business because her teenage girls required less of her time, and this former publishing powerhouse missed meaningful work. The reason she said yes to our company's opportunity was because she didn't want to let it pass her by. While she shot like a stallion out of the starting gate, fear of missing out wasn't enough to keep her business from stalling when life happened—in her case, it was both the fun things that distracted, and the heartbreak of losing her father.

It was when the stresses of her successful husband Nick's demanding career became intolerable that Amy had a breakthrough epiphany: she was sitting on a gold mine that could give her back the man she married and give her the sense of purpose she craved. That's when Amy attacked her business with an unwavering focus and commitment, leading to large jumps in organizational volume and duplication, and the unparalleled satisfaction of leading a fast-growing team to Lexus-earning volume, along with an income that set Nick free and led him to work with her. Together they've reached the top level in our company and are fulfilled by the daily impact they get to have on others.

Our WHY's evolve along with our businesses, and the key to consistent growth and not stalling out is to continually check in with yourself and your priorities. My WHY started out as a desire to escape the billable hour jail, and to create an income that would allow me to earn money even when I wasn't working (passive income). Once I was able to say goodbye to my PR career, I wanted to set John free from the confines of his fee-for-service medical practice. Once that happened, my WHY became much bigger.

> Our WHY's evolve along with our businesses, and the key to consistent growth and not stalling out is to continually check in with yourself and your priorities.

For the next three years, I saw my third WHY every time I logged onto the backend business management site our company provides us. A picture of Nate and Bebe in the bathtub with big smiles on their faces and sparkles of mischief in their eyes, with the words:

"To have the time and economic freedom to show Nate and Bebe all life has to offer, and to teach them to develop their entrepreneurial spirit to reach the highest heights and make the world a better place. And to be a change agent to help others become the best versions of themselves."

I dug deep to come up with this WHY, and it held true until our income reached six figures a month. By then, we had the time and economic freedom to do everything we wanted for our family, and we were helping others do the same. Clearly, Nate and Bebe were learning to develop an entrepreneurial spirit—they were surrounded by proof that if you work really hard at something you're passionate about, that's of value to others, it's possible to have fulfilling work while also having a life. We've had to remind both kids that it's not the norm for all families to have both parents home and accessible nearly all the time, and that perks like we enjoy don't come with a conventional job. The kids' skewed reality really hit home when one night at the dinner table John and I were talking about a friend who got a promotion at his corporate job. Bebe asked, "When is he getting his free Lexus?"

But if I was going to wake up every day still wanting to build our business, I had to find a new WHY. It became about others—not just empowering more people to become who they were destined to be, but also about being able to put significant resources toward helping women and children around the world to have access to the basics we enjoy every day: full tummies, access to health care, and empowerment programs to step into their greatness. That's enough for me to chew on for years to come, and my husband too. Which is why we bound out of bed nearly every day wanting to keep building this sucker.

As you think about your WHY, or rethink it, remember that it's ok to be selfish about what you want. That can be a hard mindset shift, especially for women, since we're programmed to be so damn selfless, and do so much for others. Yet a lot of the WHYs that I've talked about prove that doing for yourself and doing for others don't have to be mutually exclusive. Deep down, Tracy Willard wanted to be the one to save her family, and Amy wanted to set her husband free. I had the audacity to want it all—for me, for John, for our kids, for those on our team who want to run with us, and for the causes we're passionate about.

I think one of the biggest reasons many people can't find their real WHY—the one that will make them get uncomfortable, stretch and grow, and consistently show up—is because they don't dig deep enough. It really is like peeling an onion. As you explore your WHY keep asking yourself "Why is that?" For example, one of our business partners first declared that she wanted to earn more money. I started peeling, "Why is that?" So she could build an emergency fund. More peeling, "Why do you want an emergency fund?" To know she's safe. "Why will that make you safe?" Because the last time she was married, her husband left her with nothing, and in her current marriage she could be left in the same awful situation. "So I'm hearing that your real WHY is to make sure that you can always take care of yourself and put the power of your future in your hands. Is that right?" "Yes," she said, as she cried. Simply wanting to earn more money wasn't going to be enough to get this very busy working mom to consistently show up in spite of inevitable challenges. But her real WHY is powerful enough, and as a result, she's on her way to building something that will make her feel safe and empowered.

Another reason people can't figure out their WHY is because they've stopped dreaming. It's so easy to get mired in what is that we stop dreaming about what could be. Or if you haven't stopped dreaming, maybe you've stopped believing that it's possible to actually realize your dreams. If you don't believe it can happen, you don't dare go for it, let alone dream about it.

No matter what stage your life or business is in, isn't it time you gave yourself permission to dream again? Isn't it time you let yourself believe those dreams can come true? I'm living proof, as are thousands of people on our team, that whatever your dreams are, because this profession offers so much, you should be dreaming bigger. So what is it that you want for you? That's your WHY.

> No matter what stage your life or business is in, isn't it time you gave yourself permission to dream again?

Goals: Eat the elephant one bite at a time.

Once you know your reason WHY, then you've got to set goals that will lead you to achieving your WHY. Now there are effective and ineffective ways to set goals. The effective way is to take a big goal (the elephant) and break it down into bite-sized steps to make it more do-able.

At this point, I'd be remiss if I didn't mention the tried and true, gold standard of goal setting that transcends network marketing. I don't know who came up with this, but SMART goals are where it's at. Your goals must be Specific, Measurable, Achievable, Realistic and Time-bound.

A specific goal has a much greater chance of being attained than a general one. And when you break your specific goal down into bite-sized steps, it has an even better chance of being achieved. To set your specific goal, answer the three "W" questions:

* **What** do I want to accomplish?
* **When** do I want to accomplish it?
* **Why** do I want to accomplish it?

For example, a general goal would be, I want to earn back my investment. But a specific goal would be, I want to earn back my investment by the end of my first full month so I have a powerful first month story and can pay my credit card balance.

A measurable goal can be, uh, measured. For example, you've got $1500 in credit card debt that you want to pay off. A goal must also be achievable, and what I love in our profession is that pretty much every goal you come up with can be achieved with consistent hard work. Setting realistic goals is important because, while you can achieve most anything you set your mind to; you've got to be realistic about how long it will take you. This depends on how much time you're willing and able to spend on your business. For example, if you have a goal of replacing your $10,000 monthly salary in six months, but you're only willing or able to carve out six hours a week for your business, it's probably not going to happen on that timeline.

But don't let this discourage you from making stretch goals—those are different than unrealistic ones. This business grows fastest when you keep making stretch goals for yourself and your team. What's the worst that could happen? You shoot for the moon and land among the stars. Not too shabby.

Of course, you must make your goals time-bound, because a goal without a timeline is just a dream. When you're working on a deadline your sense of urgency increases, which will reduce procrastination, and will get you to the finish line that much quicker.

While your WHY can't be just about the money, monetary goals are a tangible way to measure your progress, and to track how effectively you're advancing your business and getting to your WHY. I happen to have been personally driven by a combination of monetary milestones and running after the incentives provided by our company. Dangle an incentive—cash, trip, bling—in front of me to run for, and come hell or high water, I'm gonna get it. Your company likely designs the incentives to get you to do the business building that helps you to advance in income and title, so whenever you have the chance to run after an incentive, just do it. Make it a goal and put a visual representation of the incentive in a place where you'll see it often.

> **A public declaration makes you accountable like nothing else.**

I'm a big believer in the power of writing down your goals and declaring them in as public a forum as you can possibly bear. This makes them real, and a public declaration makes you accountable like nothing else. It's also the next step in actually believing that they're possible. And that belief can make it so. Ok, I may be getting a little woo woo, but I've seen this happen too many times for myself, my husband, and members of our team, not to be a believer. So just stay with me. According to Pam Grout in E^2, we can manifest anything we want, simply by setting the intention. As Grout writes, "When you throw a tennis ball in the air, you can count on it coming down. Intention is just like that tennis ball. It comes back just the way you send it out."

How else could we explain the power of the dream board? Which I highly recommend you do and encourage all members of your team to do too. I have so many examples of pictures of goals and dreams pinned to a corkboard that end up becoming reality. Like the picture of a boat on the azure blue water that was pinned to the goal board of my dear friend and business partner, Bridget Cavanaugh. An almost identical picture appeared five years later in the brochure for a trip we earned to Greece. If you like the sound of all this and you want to tap into your inner woo woo, E^2 is the next book you should read, after you completely devour this one, of course.

With each bite-sized SMART goal achieved, your confidence builds. If my first SMART goal was to earn six-figures or retire John from clinical medicine, it would have certainly been too much to bite off. I would have choked on that elephant. But I could focus that first year on smaller, incremental goals: reaching out to three new people a day, bringing three, three-way calls a week to my upline, adding new business partners and customers every single month, paying the mortgage, then hitting the first significant promotion, then matching my PR consulting income, then beating it, then earning an incentive trip to the Wine Country, then earning the Top Recruiter Award at our company's convention, then matching John's income.

If you ask Tracy if she started her business thinking about earning a shiny new Lexus and moving back to her native Southern California to live by the beach, she would tell you absolutely not. "I had to start with putting food on the table, then making more money than my teaching job was paying so I could quit and spend more time on my business and with my girls." Then she focused on getting out of debt.

Amy Byrd, another close friend and seven-figure earner on our team, had a clear escalation of goals leading to achieving her WHY of a lucrative career that could provide her complete flexibility to be with her two "monkeys"—that's what she calls her adorable son and daughter. When she started her business, Amy's immediate goal was to earn a return on her investment in her first 30 days because she needed the room back on her credit card. Finances were that tight for this former pharmaceutical rep and her real estate developer husband. Amy's longer-term goals were time-bound, but the timelines got shorter as things went from bad to worse with the land development projects her husband was involved in, and her family of four found themselves living in her parents' basement.

Once she hit the first major promotion, she then shifted her goals to "walking the walk" for her team. "I wanted to show my team that advancement in title/promotions/trips/cars was all attainable. If I could do it, they could do it." The flexibility still allowed Amy to guard her most precious asset—time with her kids—as she worked her way out of the basement and into a beautiful new home and among the ranks of the very top leaders in our entire company.

John and I have both learned that while we need to set a goal and work toward it, that's not where our day-to-day focus should be. Instead, we focus on the **process** of reaching the goal. For example, if your goal is to add three new business partners a month, ask the Universe (or whomever or whatever you ask things of) to bring more people into your life who you can share this with. Asking sets your intention. And then take advantage of every opportunity that presents itself to share about your business and your products or services. Every time you run into someone picking your child up from school. The friendly stranger you're sitting next to at the restaurant (don't worry; we'll talk about how to do this the right way later on). The long lost friend you notice in your newsfeed on Facebook. Share with everyone the Universe brings into your life.

> **Take advantage of every opportunity that presents itself to share about your business and your products or services.**

Because if you have enough conversations, you'll find the people who want to become your customers and those who want to join you in business. Fall in love with the process, and it will lead you to achieve your goals. Then 12 months from now, if you've stayed focused, you'll look back on all you've accomplished, how much you've grown, and I expect, you'll have developed a real love for the journey.

How badly do you want it?

This is what separates the talkers from the doers. It's one thing to say you want to build a business, identify your WHY and set goals that will get you there. But it's a whole other can of tomatoes to actually BUILD it.

The how-badly-you-want-it loops back to your WHY. Again, it's got to be big enough that you're willing to give up things like TV (I didn't watch television the first two years of my business unless I was on a piece of cardiovascular equipment), People magazine (yes, even in the bathroom I was reading personal and professional development), cooking every night (I came to love the concept of "meal assembly" so I must give a huge shout out to Costco). You've also got to get buy-in from the people who share your life, like your husband and your kids.

As we've already established, growing a six- and seven-figure business takes consistency and talking to people every single day. Because not everyone you bring on board will be coachable or have a strong enough WHY to keep them motivated—you'll have team members who do nothing, and you'll have others who quit. This is a business of attrition. It's a numbers game. If you're not personally adding at least two new business partners a month, you're not insulating yourself from the attrition. So you're actually contracting and not expanding.

You may feel like you want to quit, but you've got to commit to work 18-24 months as hard and as smart as you can. As I was building my business in those first two years, I kept telling myself this famous quote [author unknown]: "Entrepreneurship is living a few years of your life like most people won't, so that you can spend the rest of your life like most people can't."

This "how bad do you want it" question is really about pain and pleasure. As humans, we avoid anything that feels like pain and instantly take action toward things we believe will make us feel good, or that will give us pleasure. Now you can certainly view spending time building your business, learning how to talk to people, and taking No's and disappointments as painful.

But what if you could coach yourself and others to wire your brain to link pain to **NOT taking action** in your business, and massive pleasure to **taking action**? I'm talking about working with the deepest part of your subconscious. Yes, it's getting deep now. Stay with me.

> **What if you could coach yourself and others to wire your brain to link pain to NOT taking action in your business, and massive pleasure to taking action?**

Has it ever felt like lifting 500 pounds to pick up your five-ounce smart phone and call people? Or to say five words to start a conversation with the person next to you in line at Starbucks?

Is so, you simply need to rewire your brain so that **not taking action** is extremely painful, and **taking action** lights you up inside. When you do, you'll find you don't have to rely on sheer willpower as much. You'll simply want to do it.

Now, you may be thinking, "Romi, you said you're a no-BS kinda girl, but this sounds like a whole lot of horseshit to me." I was born and raised in Montana, and I assure you, I know horseshit from a mile away, and this ain't it!

You *can* rewire your brain. It's a scientific fact. There was even a phenomenal article in the Wall Street Journal summarizing what personal development guru Tony Robbins and others have been teaching for years. It just took neuropsychiatry a little longer to catch up. The article said, "The mainstream view in neuroscience and medicine today is that the living brain is actually 'neuroplastic'—meaning that its 'circuits' are constantly changing in response to what we actually do out in the world. As we think, perceive, form memories, or learn new skills, the connections between brain cells also change and strengthen. Far from being hard-wired, the brain has circuits that very rapidly form, unform and reform." [Doidge, N. "Our Amazingly Plastic Brains".]

Holy crap! Are you getting how amazing this is and what it can mean for your business and your life? The brain constantly changes based on what we think and do. We can change how our brains are wired! This opens up a whole new spectrum of possibilities, doesn't it?

I'm going to help you "wire yourself" or "rewire yourself" for success. I'm going to have you do an exercise that I had a group of my team members do in my coaching series.

In doing so, you'll be training your brain that the pleasure you seek is in **doing the work** to build your business and reach your WHY. And the pain that you, oh human, so desperately want to avoid is in **not doing the work** to build your business and reach your WHY.

After you do your homework, we'll hit the next chapter. You'll get a break from woo woo for a bit as we focus on a skill you've been honing since you were a kid writing to Santa. I know you're intrigued, but do not move forward until you've done your homework. Be coachable. Jeesh.

Get in Action

Please take out a notebook or journal and answer the following questions:

1) What is your WHY? (Remember to peel the onion to get to your real WHY.)

2) Why is this so important to you? Get really specific here. How do you see this changing your life, affecting your family, helping you get where you want to be long-term?

3) If you don't achieve your WHY, what's the pain you'll experience? In other words, what's the cost you'll pay in your life by not taking action to build this business? Really flesh out this part. What will you and your family miss out on in life? How will this affect your confidence and your self-esteem?

4) Look ahead five years into the future. If you don't achieve your WHY, where will you be and what will you have given up, all because you didn't follow through and take action on what was important?

Read this every day for three weeks. I found it really helpful to read it first thing in the morning, even before my feet hit the floor, to help set my intention for the day. You may decide to do it before you go to sleep. It doesn't matter when you do it, as long as you do it. Every day for 21 days.

CHAPTER 3

Your List Is Your Life: Make It a Long One

Alright, you've established or re-established the founda-tion of your business—your WHY —and you've set some short-term goals. Now it's time to focus on the lifeline of your business: Your List.

Your list truly is your life in this business, so make sure it's a long one. It's a living, breathing thing that you should be consulting, updating and tweaking daily. The sooner you get in the habit of thinking of Your List in this way, the sooner it will become a valuable asset to your business.

Another way to think of it is like a bank account. As you make withdrawals (take people off your list), you've got to make deposits (always adding new people). So we're going to talk about how to make deposits to your list every day. I'll show you how to work with your list over time to keep it organized so you can focus more efficiently on income producing activity (IPA) and growing your business faster. Do what I'm about to teach you and your list will never get anemic.

Create your Master List.

The best thing you can do for yourself and your future busi-ness partners is to keep a very thorough Master List. This list includes every human you know, whether it's a close relationship or acquaintance. The key is not to prejudge who goes on this list. We have no idea who will be interested in what we have to offer. Many make the mistake of segmenting their list by prejudging what their network will be interested in. Putting people into predetermined categories of "Product User" and "Team Member" is a fruitless exercise. First, there's no way for us to predict who will be interested in what part of our business. The majority of our monthly income comes from the teams of three people I never thought would be interested in starting their own turn-key enterprise. Heck, I've had countless people tell me that they never would've guessed I'd ever be interested in something like this. Second, categorizing people will consciously or unconsciously cause you to tailor your conversation and you'll unknowingly choose how that person will be involved. As I'll teach you, you'll be much more effective if you lead with the business and default to the products.

> The best thing you can do for yourself and your future business partners is to keep a very thorough master list.

I coach our new business partners on their very first day in business to take a pad and paper and write down "everyone you know with skin," since our business is skincare and it always makes them chuckle. Then, I have them put stars by their **Top 30 Dream Teamers**. These are the people they would love to work with, for whatever reason. Maybe they have a track record of proven success. Maybe they have magnetic personalities. Maybe they are influencers in their networks. Maybe they just get shiz done. Or maybe they're just so damn much fun you'd think it would be an absolute blast to work with them. Now, keep in mind, you have no earthly idea if they'd actually *want* to do this, but that's not the point. You're identifying them as part of your Dream Team, just like in a fantasy football league, because you're now the CEO and you can choose to "hire" whomever you want. Whether they accept is up to them.

I also ask them to identify who on their list would be part of a "Dirt List." Simply put, these are the people who love and support you so much that if you were selling dirt they would want to support you. I didn't coin this term by the way, I heard it at a training and thought it was so adorable and brilliant that I adopted it. This list will likely include your mom, dad, grandparents, sister, and your BFF. I've seen how helpful making Dirt List calls with your upline team member can be when you're brand new. These calls are a great way to start learning from your business partner right away, quickly putting the whole "earn as you learn" method to use. It also gets your first calls under your belt, and shows you that it's really fun and won't kill you. I've seen it help newbies add their first few customers, business partners, and referrals right out of the gate. It's ok that you don't know much yet; your business partner does most of the talking. For details on how to actually execute these suckers, hold tight. We'll cover that in Chapter 10: "Three-Way, Anyone?"

But I can't come up with more than 25 people.

Or more than 40 or 55 or 100...we've all heard some shockingly low number for humans who have been on the planet for 20 or more years. I'm calling BS on this one, and it's actually been proven to be total BS.

A *New York Times* article reported that the average American knows about 600 people, according to researchers at Columbia University. Tian Zheng and colleagues posed a series of questions to a representative sample of 1,500 Americans: How many people do you know named Kevin? How many named Karen? How many named Shawn or Sean, Brenda, Keith or Rachel? After adjusting for various factors, including that names are not evenly represented across different ages in the population, they determined that participants knew an average of 8.4 people with those names. Social Security records suggest that 1.4% of the population has one of these names, and 8.4 divided by 1.4% is 600 people. [Gelman, A. (2013). "The Average Person Knows How Many People?", The New York Times.]

Even if you're skeptical of this number or don't even understand the math, let's look at social network research from decades earlier. The same article reported that H. Russell Bernard and Peter Killworth estimated that the average American knows 290 people. This lower number could be because the names they used were common ones, like Michael and Robert, and research shows that people with common names are harder to recall than those with slightly more exotic ones, like Sean and Rachel. But it could also be because the recent rise of social media has not only increased people's networks, but also kept people from our past more in our lives and more likely for us to recall. Keep in mind, there's no indication that the research volunteers were people whose professions required them to cultivate their networks, meaning the number will be much lower than people like us whose gig is about being an active, social human, and making new friends all the time. If that's never been you, it will be you. You can do this.

Not satisfied with the numbers provided by the people who've made a career of researching social networks? Let's look at weddings then. TheKnot.com 2013 Real Weddings Study reports that the average wedding has 138 guests. Also according to these wedding gurus, ten to 20% of those invited won't attend. So the average invite list is 151.8 to 165.6. Since we can't have a fraction of a person (although I have met people who have a fraction of a personality, and thus would not be a good choice for this biz), let's agree that the average number of people one feels close enough to in order to snag an invite to one of the most important events of his or her life is 152 to 165. So please don't tell me that you don't know at least 200 humans on the planet. And that's just for starters.

Here's the great news: no matter how many or few people are on your initial master list, you'll continually be adding to that list. You'll likely think of new people every day, and at least once a month you should sit down and methodically add people to your list. A great way to do that is to jog your memory by looking at the following categories you may know on the next page. Try coming up with four new names in each category during your monthly session. Do that and you'll have more than 100 new people to reach out to.

> You'll likely think of new people every day, and at least once a month you should sit down and methodically add people to your list.

When you think you've exhausted these categories, try what the researchers have done. Go through names, starting with "A" through "Z" and write down those who come to mind.

If after all these exercises, you or your newbie still can't think of more than 30 or so humans you know on the planet, then you probably don't like people enough for this profession. So stick with being a happy product user and hand over that list of people you do know to the person who brought you into the biz.

Get in Action

Let's start jogging your memory right now. Spend 15 minutes writing down four names in each category and add them to your Master List.

* Community leaders, movers and shakers
* People you went to school with (elementary, middle, high, college)
* Church, synagogue or temple
* Friends of friends
* My spouse's or boyfriend's network
* Past and present work colleagues
* Dinner parties, bridal showers, weddings, graduations
* People who provide you services: accountants, Fed-Ex Delivery, nail tech, plumber
* Professionals: educators, health care professionals, lawyers, real estate agents
* Non-profit boards and volunteers
* Social media contacts: Facebook, LinkedIn, Instagram
* Chamber of Commerce members/events
* Moms' groups, stay-at-home moms
* Groups: book clubs, bunco groups, happy hour groups
* People with hobbies: golfers, tennis players, gardeners, equestrians, cyclists, hikers
* Political activist groups
* Parents of kids' classmates
* Parents in all kids' activities (sports, clubs, religious school)

* Teachers, coaches, instructors, mentors
* People on trains, planes, and automobiles
* Active military or military spouses
* Swimming pool loungers and coffee shop regulars
* Neighbors and former neighbors
* People who sell stuff: real estate, cars, retail
* People who love the arts: symphony, opera, fine art, ballet patrons
* People whose business you support or have supported
* People who get things done
* My brother's network, my sister's network
* My parents' networks

Create your chicken list.

If you don't reach out to your chicken list, the people you're too afraid to talk to will end up on someone else's team, as someone else's customer, or someone else's connector to a runner. Given the growth rate of some companies and our profession as a whole, this isn't conjecture; it's fact. So get over your damn self, quit making up stories in your head about what the chicken list people will say or think or do, and just take action.

Let's be honest, if the people on your Chicken List are such studs that they intimidate the hell out of you or cause you to make up apocalyptic stories in your head, aren't they precisely the people you want on your team or at least as evangelists for your products or connecting you to their networks?

I implore you to reach out right away to every single person who makes your belly do flip flops or makes you want to hurl when you think about approaching them. After all, the very reason they're on your chicken list is probably why you'd want them on your team. I promise that you won't die. Just do it.

There was one person who was on my chicken list when I started. She was the last boss I ever had, and let's just say my departure wasn't all sunshine and roses. Even though we parted on not-so-great terms, there was no denying this woman had serious smarts, business chops and people skills, and she should've been one of the first people I called. Yet while I wasn't worried what others thought of what I was doing, I was really nervous to tell her. Honestly, I can't quite remember why. I think it had something to do with how on the outside it seemed like she was so in love with her marketing career and owning an agency, and maybe I feared that she would think I gave up or was crazy to want to get out of PR (or some other story I was making up in my head). In reality I had no idea what she would think. None of us know what anyone is thinking, so all the time and energy you spend speculating is a waste.

> None of us know what anyone is thinking, so all the time and energy you spend speculating is a waste.

One day, about three months after I launched my business, she called to see if I'd be willing to do some media relations contract work for a client of hers. "I'm so sorry I can't help you, but I'm shutting down my PR career. I've found something far too fun and far too lucrative," flew out of my mouth. "But thanks so much for asking. Why don't I send you the contact info for someone I think would be perfect. Sound good?"

"Sure, that would be great," she stammered, and we said our goodbyes. Less than an hour later she emailed to ask me if I'd meet her for coffee that afternoon. She had poked around on Facebook and saw what I was up to and wanted to talk about it. At our meeting she told me all the reasons she should be a part of this. My chicken lister was recruiting herself! After our coffee talk, she enrolled. It was ten days before our company's first national convention, and she went with me. Her name is Bridget Cavanaugh, and she has become one of our team's, and the entire company's, MVPs. She's a seven-figure earner and is one of my most trusted and effective power partners. And this business also healed a frayed friendship, exponentially growing our mutual respect, and developing a deep love for each other and our families.

I shudder to think of what would've happened if she didn't need some PR help, because I had no plans to call her anytime soon, and one of my other teammates in our town could've easily reached out to her.

Don't be chicken shit. It could cost you millions and keep you from living the life you really want.

Manage your Master List.

Writing your list on a pad of paper is a great way for a newbie to start. It's easy and duplicable. But it's not an efficient enough system for the long haul. Once my new business partner gets through her first dozen conversations, I encourage her to come up with a better list management system. Since you'll want to take notes on when you've talked to them, what they said, next steps, and any other important notes to use in follow-up, there has to be room for that info and the ability to edit.

Some business builders love note cards filed in boxes that are separated by dividers with dates as to when to next follow-up. Others swear by a notebook with notes after every name, or a note on their phone (although it scares me to death how easily that could be lost). Very popular on our team are Excel spreadsheets. There are new apps being developed for list management. As for me, I've worked with a Word doc with an embedded table for years because, honestly, I'm faster with Word than Excel. Either one allows for easy "find" functions that allow you to search for the "flight attendant" on your list when there's another success story just released in your company blog about a flight attendant who retired because she surpassed her day job earnings.

No matter what you end up using, understand that you may have lists that you create all over the place. We can't always dictate when our memory will be jogged, after all. Just promise yourself that you'll take all those names scribbled on the backs of envelopes or in random notebooks, or in notes on your phone, and transfer them to your Master List. You'll be so grateful for this simple practice in discipline.

Add to your list every day.

The key to adding to your list all the time is to get out of your house and make new friends every day. Go where the people are. Instead of driving through the outside bank window or the Starbucks drive-thru, go inside and stand in line where you'll meet other humans. If you work from home, take turns working at different cafes and chitchat with people next to you. Get involved in hobbies that involve people. Accept invitations. When you're on an airplane, never fall asleep or put ear buds in until you've had thorough conversations with all the people around you. Keep falling in love with people—connecting with them, learning about them and discovering whether you have something of value for them.

> **The key to adding to your list all the time is to get out of your house and make new friends every day.**

I get how hard this can be. It's still hard for me sometimes. I'm what's considered an introverted extrovert, or an extroverted introvert (I can never remember which one). But what it means is that while I love people and get energy from being with them, after a while I just need to be alone. Blissfully alone. Yet what I've learned is that as long as I take little snippets of quiet alone time for myself to recharge—even as little as 15 minutes of meditation or reading—it makes it easier to do the level of socializing required to flourish in our people-centric business. I accept every invitation I get for a social outing unless I have a really good excuse (like the kids are sick or I've got an even better invite). Even this morning I wrestled with an invitation for a "Mom's Day Out" at a glass-blowing shop. I will be coming off a week of houseguests, followed by a week of ski travel with John and the kids, bumping up against month end for our business and trying to get this book done. So my knee-jerk emotional reaction was, "Oh good God, no way I'm doing one more thing." But then my seasoned business-builder brain kicked in and looked at all the other people invited. "That's a lot of fresh meat," I told myself and clicked Yes to RSVP.

I get it; you're tired. It's snowing. You've been talking to people all week. Your kids have sucked out every remaining bit of energy you had. Your couch and your favorite movie are calling you. But remember how badly you want this. And get your ass out there.

Oh, the days of getting your ass out there when you're looking like a mess? They're over. Because we take our business with us wherever we go—we need to be ready to make new friends, we've got to be presentable all the time. Don't get me wrong, I'm not suggesting you need to be perfectly coiffed and dressed to the nines every time you go out the door. You simply want to feel confident and make the person you encounter think you have your act somewhat together. Simply put, if you look like hell, no one is going to want to use what you have to offer or build a business so they can have your life.

So once you're out there, what do you do with all the people you meet? Start friendly conversations and see if the person responds in kind. If they don't, then we know they wouldn't be any good at what we do. But if they smile and engage in conversation, they're a personable human, and you should ask them some questions to learn a bit about them. Your intention shouldn't be to vomit all over them about your business. This is not an instant-gratification process. Instead find a reason to exchange contact info so you can follow-up with them another time. I call this "getting digits."

I always love to ask someone if they're a local. If they're not, they usually tell where they originally hail from. That leaves a great opportunity to mention, "Hey, my business is expanding to [wherever they're from]. I'd love to pick your brain some-time about who you know there who might be a great fit for what I do. Let's exchange contact info." Then you go home, add that person as a Facebook friend, and put in your calendar a reminder to call them in the next day or so.

I also meet a lot of new people by offering to be a resource for them. If a conversation leads to someone who is looking for a baby sitter or a dog groomer, I offer to send them some recommendations. I genuinely enjoy being a resource for peo-ple, and this also allows me to get their contact info and keep in contact with them. Again, this isn't instant gratification. It's about building a relationship. I'll help them and then I can ask to pick their brain about their network to see if someone might be a fit for my business.

When you're out and about, you're bound to run into peo-ple you know. Have a lovely conversation and then throw in,

"I was actually going to reach out to you. I've started a new business, and I'd love to pick your brain. Can I give you a call tomorrow morning? Which time works better for you, nine or 10:30?"

Another key skill is keeping your ears open. Now that you're building a business with products or services and a business model that can help people, listen for opportunities to offer up solutions to someone's problem. If you're chatting with a parent at the side of the soccer field and she admits to missing the last three games because of work, you should respond, "Maybe you should take a look at what I do. You might be able to build a side business that could set you free from your rigid work schedule. I don't know if you'll be interested, but it's probably worth a look. Let's exchange contact info, and I'll give you a call tomorrow night. What time will you be free after the kids go to bed?"

If you meet someone at the pool on vacation and they complain that this is the first trip they've taken in years because of too little time and money, you respond, "Maybe you should take a look at what I do. You could build a side biz that could fill vacation funds and even one day give you more time freedom. I don't know if it'll be a good fit, but it's worth a look. Let's exchange contact info and follow up when we get back to our real lives."

Listen for opportunities to offer up solutions to someone's problem.

The same concept applies for problems you may hear that your products can solve. Try listening more and you'll be amazed at how many opportunities there are to share.

I love watching the top recruiters on our team and how they take their business with them wherever they go. They view the entire world as full of possibilities. It's not that they walk around vomiting all over people about our business and products. But they are so genuinely friendly and make new friends wherever they go. Like one of our biggest business builders, Kim Krause. Kim makes friends wherever she goes. She loves talking to people and starts conversations with no agenda other than to connect with other humans. If she gets a tepid response, she doesn't take it personally and doesn't let it deter her from being her authentically friendly self. Kim has met future business partners and customers on airplanes, at resorts while on vacation, running errands, at her kids' activities and at restaurants. All these conversations have expanded her network and contributed to her seven-figure income.

The world is full of people you know and can meet, so you never have to run out of people to talk to. Keep reading so I can teach you how to use this list. Because the longest list in the world isn't going to do you any good if you don't reach out to the people on it!

CHAPTER 4

What's Your Story?

Before I can tell you how to talk to people about your business and your products or services, we first have to make sure you know how to talk about yourself. In our business, we're paid storytellers. So the better you are at telling your story, the more successful you'll be. It's important to know how to craft and revise your own story, and how to edit your team members' stories as well. You also need to learn how to adapt your story to connect with the person you're talking to, to help show what's in it for them. So I'll explain to you why you should build an always-growing story library.

When we share about our businesses, we talk about our respective company stories. Stories about our products or services and why they're different, the awards and rankings, media attention, and more. If you're telling those stories right, all that should be undisputable fact. The last thing you want to do is tell stories full of bullshit. If you feel the need to embellish these stories, then you're either not well enough informed about your company or you're with the wrong company.

While facts are important, they're not enough, not by a long shot. As the saying goes, "Facts tell, but stories sell." It's true. Humans act on emotion. Any psychology journal will confirm that humans are not rational beings, but rationalizing beings. We decide we want to buy something, and then we go looking for reasons why it's a good idea. We decide to start a business and then we go looking for reasons why it's a good idea.

> **We're paid storytellers.**
> **So the better you are at**
> **telling your story, the**
> **more successful you'll be.**

A compelling story is what's going to allow you to draw them in emotionally. Capturing their attention with why you wanted to start a business of your very own, what you've done with it (or are going to do with it), and how someone like them can do something like this, will create an emotional connection. A well-crafted story is **fact wrapped in emotion**.

First though, there's something we all must get clear on. There are many business owners who call their story their WHY. They're not the same thing. As we discussed in Chapter 2, one of the first things you do as you start your business is to declare your WHY—your reason for doing this business. You already know that your WHY has to be big enough and important enough to get you to consistently build this business, even when you're tired, discouraged, super busy, and life gets in the way.

But your WHY is not your story. It's a part of your story. So as you develop or revise your WHY and write and rewrite your story, please understand they are different things.

The elements of your story matter.

Personal short stories are formulaic, and once you nail the formula, you'll be able to not only craft your own powerful and compelling story, but you'll also be able to teach your team how to do it. Here's the formula:

1) Who you are and where you've been
2) What's happened in your life to cause you to look for something more
3) How you heard about your company and why you had to be part of it
4) What it's doing for you or going to do for you

These short stories are also **short**. We're talking 45 seconds to a minute. Truly. So once you think you've nailed it, time yourself. There are a whole lot of people in our profession walking around telling "short stories" that have them droning on for two or more minutes. Remember, the person you're talking to about your business and your products is more important than you. So tell your compelling story and then get to them and their questions. Of course, you may elaborate on certain parts of your experiences later in your discussion to answer questions or prove a point, but your story has to be quick, compelling, and with nothing redundant or superfluous in it.

When I started my business, here was my short story. I've broken it into the corresponding short story elements:

1) Who you are and where you've been
   I've been tied to the billable hour and at the beck and call of my clients my entire career—first as a lawyer and then as a PR exec.

2) What's happened in your life to cause you to look for something more
   But as a mom of two little ones, I want more flexibility, to own my own schedule and to make more money to get further ahead. It's a tall order for a working mom, but I've found a way to have it.

3) How you heard about your company and why you had to be part of it
   My PR client introduced me to (my company). She was funding the business she hired me to promote through her side gig with (my company). I immediately recognized this was a way to build my exit strategy from Corporate America to the lifestyle I really want.

4) What it's doing for you or going to do for you
I'm excited to grow a team and a customer base around my PR practice, the kids, and all the other things on my plate, to create the lifestyle I really want. And I'm excited to help others have more options too.

Here's how it all flowed together:
I've been tied to the billable hour and at the beck and call of my clients my entire career—first as a lawyer and then as a PR exec. But as a mom of two little ones, I want more flexibility, to own my own schedule and to make more money to get further ahead. It's a tall order for a working mom, but I've found a way to have it. My PR client introduced me to (my company). She was funding the business she hired me to promote through her side gig with (my company). I immediately recognized this was a way to build my exit strategy from Corporate America. I'm excited to grow a team and a customer base around my PR practice, the kids, and all the other things on my plate, to create the lifestyle I really want. And I'm excited to help others have more options too.

What have I done in that story? I've drawn them into my life—where I was, what I was feeling, what I wanted, and also where this was going to take me. Were you drawn in? Was there anything in there that you could relate to? Most likely. Not all of it, of course, but certainly some aspects.

Could I have said a lot more? Sure. But at 49 seconds, it gives a strong foundation for our discussion. If the person I'm talking to is a mom or a career person (or former career person) who has dealt with that elusive life balance we all seek, or someone looking to get further ahead, or who knows people like this, I'll make enough of a connection with them to get them to sit up and actively listen.

Here's what you should leave out.

What you leave out of your story is just as important as what you put in. Make sure to leave this stuff on the cutting room floor.

Things that aren't essential to your story.

I call this the extra fluff that doesn't really add anything. I was a journalism major and we were always taught if you have written 100 words but you can say it in 50, then cut it. It's the same thing with our stories.

To cut this extra fluff out you have to be ruthless with your editing. I know it's hard because we're all attached to our stories—it's who we are. That's why it's helpful to have your upline take a stab at it, as well as someone not in the business who can give you an objective edit such as your husband, your BFF, or your mom.

Suggesting behavior you don't want them to do.

This happens all the time and makes me cringe. Remember that with everything you say and do you are teaching people how to do this business. So when your story includes "I heard about my company and I immediately researched everything I could about it over the next two weeks," you're shooting yourself in the foot. Really, do you want people to do that? Don't you want them to review what you send them in an information email and get on a three-way call and make a decision?

> Remember that with everything you say and do you are teaching people how to do this business.

What about this head-scratcher, "I used the products for two years before I became a rep for the company." Cue blood-curdling scream! If you were a product or service user first, I'm not telling you to lie about it. I'm just telling you not to mention it. Why plant any seed that they should use the products before starting their business? You can sing the praises of the product or service without implying that someone should be simply a product or service user before building a business. In fact, in our company and especially on our team, we have thousands and thousands of people who relied on the clinical studies, jaw-dropping before and after pictures, success stories, and our 60-day guarantee to jump in without using the products first. If the fact that you fell in love with the products first was instrumental in you joining the business, you can include something like, "I loved the idea of being able to have the best skin of my life (giving my body the best nutrition or whatever your product or service is) and getting paid for it."

Personal product testimonials.

I'm a big believer that product stories shouldn't be included in your short story, whether you're brand new or an accomplished veteran. If you include a personal product testimonial, it will suggest to prospects and new business builders that they need to have their own personal product story before starting to share about the business and the products. That's why my short story I used when I launched my business didn't include one. Heck, I started talking to people before my business kit arrived!

A personal products testimonial, if you have one yet, can come out in other parts of your discussion. More on this a little later.

An ending that doesn't contain quantifiables.

Our short stories should all build to a compelling climax. When you're brand new, your story builds to what you think this business will do for you. As your business grows, you'll be able to share what I like to call "quantifiables." Ok, so I sort of made up that word. According to the dictionary "quantifiable" is an adjective, but I've turned it into a noun because it describes perfectly what should be at the end of your short story. Simply put, quantifiables are the numbers that show growth and what the business is doing for you.

By quantifiables, I'm not referring to all the incredible people you now get to work with, or the active social life this business has given you, or how this business has taught you to break out of your comfort zone. That's all fabulous stuff and you may decide to include that in your 45 seconds to a minute. However, the biggest questions people have when considering a business like ours is some variation of "Does this business model actually work and can I do it too?" So while some people may in fact join you for the warm and fuzzy side benefits, which have been amazing, the majority will want to commit to their own turn-key business to pay for something. To quote the legendary Cuba Gooding Jr. in the movie *Jerry Maguire*, "Show Me The Money!"

In our business, the Code of Ethics of the Direct Selling Association (DSA) prohibits us from disclosing the actual dollar amount of our earnings. However, we can paint the picture of how we're growing and what we're earning through illustrating and explaining what that paycheck is allowing us to do over what time frame. Great examples include what you're able to pay for ("I'm covering all the kids' activities."), or how it stacks up to your job or former job ("I've been in business just ten months and I'm already earning half of what I earn in my full-time job.").

After my first month in business, I was able to add some very compelling quantifiables. "After just a month in business, I have a group of happy customers whose skin is changing; I earned back my investment, and made our car payment."

After my second month my story built to this crescendo, "In my first month, I was profitable and made my car payment. Now, after just two months working my business around my busy life, I've grown a team of six in Montana and California, I have happy customers in four states, I've earned bonuses and three promotions, and just paid our mortgage!" Now those are quantifiables that get someone's attention.

If you donate time or money to charitable causes because of your business, you should include that. "Because I was able to quit my day job, I'm now able to volunteer a few hours a week at the hospital." or "I'm able to support an organization that empowers marginalized women in third-world countries." Even if philanthropy is your primary reason for building your business; however, I strongly believe you should still include the monetary quantifiables.

Your story can be a great launching point for further discussion. If the last part of your story is, "I'm able to pay all our household bills with my check, which gives us more money for our vacation fund," imagine how you could turn the conversation to the other person by asking, "If you had extra money coming in to cover living expenses, what would you love to be able to do?"

Your story will evolve.

Because your business will grow, your story will evolve. Take a few minutes and review it every month after your earnings come in. As you have more and more conversations and get more comfortable talking about your business, you'll have greater insights as to what parts of your story are most compelling and what aren't.

You'll also find that as you get more comfortable and start experiencing success, you may be willing to be more authentic with your story. I've seen many times that a business partner's first story isn't the "real" one, but it took a little while for them to be ok with the vulnerability that comes along with telling their truth. But your power lies in your truth. Every single time one of our business partners reworked her story to reveal her true story, she started attracting more people and growing faster. People are drawn to authenticity, so don't be afraid to share your real story, even before it's totally comfortable to do so.

> People are drawn to authenticity, so don't be afraid to share your real story, even before it's totally comfortable to do so.

Let's take a look at our business partner and friend Layton Griffin's story evolution. When she started her business it was: girl works in politics for a decade; girl decides to have a baby and shifts to being a stay-at-home mom (SAHM); girl gets presented this opportunity and realizes how incredible it is; girl jumps in, does well, and is excited that her husband, who loves his job, will be able to stay with it as long as he wants and not have to chase a paycheck as our needs and dreams grow. Not bad. But her close friend and fellow business MVP Lauren Myers one day pointed out to her that it was "weak sauce." Layton agreed that it was just *meh*, but argued that she didn't have some deep, dark, desperation or cause that she's driven to.

But Lauren challenged her. "Because she knows me well, Lauren reminded me that I did, in fact, have a story, and that it was just a matter of forcing myself to be more vulnerable. Which is funny, because I'm an open book, but for some reason I wasn't being open and honest when it came to this."

Layton's story then got real. "Now when I share my story it starts with the decade in politics, switching gears to being a stay-at-home mom, to then being four months pregnant with our second child when my husband had a major career upheaval. Since I'm the product of two bankers, and wasn't bringing in an income, I was terrified. In the four months my husband spent thoroughly weighting his options and searching for the best and happiest fit for him, we depleted every penny of our emergency fund. I probably wouldn't have given this opportunity as much consideration as I did when it was presented, had we not just gone through that very scary year, and were still enduring the very slow process of building that emergency savings, with now two mouths to feed and a new job that initially paid my husband considerably less than he had previously been making. But seeing how happy he was, how appreciated he was, and as a result how happy we all were, I never wanted him to be forced to leave a job that was so rewarding to chase a paycheck. This business was the opportunity to help us build back that safety net, and handle the surprise expenses that have come up. Now I've set the goal to match my husband's income, which is substantially more than the salary he left, which he is so excited about, and in the process we will have built up our savings to greater than it was when we needed it so badly just four years ago. We have security, which is invaluable."

Layton's much more connected to her story now, and she can tell that the people she is talking to are more engaged as well, which has made reach-outs more fun and a lot more productive. Her courage to be authentic and vulnerable was definitely a big contributing factor to her accelerated growth that got her cute booty into a free Lexus!

Here's how to talk about a slow start.

What if you've been doing this a while without a lot of success, but you've decided to ramp it up? Again, I always go for authenticity, so tell the truth. Maybe your truth is:

> *For the last year I've loved the wholesale discount and home-based business tax deductions, but I've treated this like a hobby. I'm surrounded by success stories of what can happen when you treat this like a business, and I'm ready to run. I'm looking for people to run with me. Are you one of them?*

Or

> *When I started, I really got in my own way. I wasn't coachable and I let fear get the best of me. But I'm surrounded by success stories of what can happen when you are coachable and follow the simple, duplicable business. And I'm not going to let fear keep me from reaching my goals.*

Adapt your story for your audience.

As you get more comfortable with your story, you'll be able to adapt it based on what you think will best connect you to each person. For example, when I'm talking to a stay-at-home mom who hasn't been in the work world for years or ever, I downplay my high-powered career and focus more on being a mom who wants to have it all. If I'm talking to someone without kids and who has no desire to have kids, I briefly touch on the fact that I'm a mom to illustrate how little free time I have, but don't focus on the emotional pull to have more flexibility for my kids.

Build your story library.

As we've discussed, one of the biggest questions your prospects have is "Can I do this?" The best way to give them confidence is to show them that someone just like them is doing it. However, you won't always be that someone just like them. So the best way to show them is through stories about other business builders. I encourage—implore you really—to get disciplined at collecting stories, just like you'd collect books if you were building a library. Your collection should include all different walks of life—men, women, couples, various ages, and a spectrum of backgrounds.

Here are just a few to add to your library:

* SAHM
* Professional with full-time job
* Working mom
* Single mom
* Lawyer
* Real estate professional
* Financial pro
* Flight attendant
* Teacher
* Social worker
* Student
* Medical professionals (doctors, physician assistants, nurses, chiropractors, massage therapists, physical therapists)
* Man (if your company is largely women-focused)
* Couple building together
* Someone who couldn't afford the starter kit but found a way, and what she did with the business
* Someone with a first and/or second month success story that shows how a quick ROI is possible

You'll be able to share these stories in conversations with your own prospects and in three-way calls. In fact, there is no greater tool to answer objections than success stories (stay tuned, we'll cover objections in Chapter 7).

I encourage you to create a culture on your team of sharing success stories. Make sure when you give recognition to your team members that you share a bit about them so

> **There is no greater tool to answer objections than success stories.**

others can add them to their libraries. Include a success story spotlight in your team newsletter or team Facebook group. If you're lucky enough to have a company blog that features your colleagues like we do (and great search functionality), read it religiously, and make sure to share relevant stories with your prospects and new business partners.

And here's a valuable side benefit to collecting these stories—you'll be constantly building your belief in your company and that you, too, can reach your goals.

What is your personal product or services story?

As we already discussed, when you first launch your business, you may not have a personal products story. In our company, it's not uncommon to be reaching out and sharing about the business and our products before we even get our kits.

When you're new and haven't used the products yet, be honest if someone asks if you're using them yet. "I can't wait for my new business kit to get here. I was so blown away by the (clinical studies/before and after pics/testimonials) that I didn't want to wait to start building a business of my own."

Once you've used the products or services, you'll have a story of your own. When you do, make sure to follow the same rules that we covered for your short story. As your company launches new products and services, use everything you can so you can personally speak to them. And just like with business short stories, collect a library of product or service stories from around your company. For example, I don't have sensitive skin, but I've been able to sell a lot of our products for sensitive skin, because I've collected stories and real results pictures from those whose skin has been transformed.

Facts tell, but stories sell. So the sooner you become good at crafting, editing and collecting stories, the better you'll be at this gig. If you're constantly feeding yourself with stories about how your company and your products are positively impacting people, you'll increase your belief and be able to inspire others too.

> **Facts tell, but stories sell. So the sooner you become good at crafting, editing and collecting stories, the better you'll be at this gig.**

CHAPTER 5

How I Talked my Way to Seven Figures and How You Can Too

We've already established that to grow a big business you're going to have to talk to a lot of people. That's what I did.

I speak from experience when I say earning a million bucks in this profession ain't easy. It's hard work. Consistent work. It takes thousands of conversations—with people you know, people you're going to meet and people your team will introduce you to. That's what I did. First, I talked my way into earning my investment back. Then I talked my way into matching my PR income. Then retiring John from clinical medicine. Ultimately I talked my way into a seven-figure income. And guess what? So can you.

So if you've gotten this far in the book, and the thought of having thousands of conversations with people makes you run for the hills, this may not be the right fit for you, and you might want to give this book to one of your team members. Before you do, let's dig a bit deeper.

The whole "thousands of conversations" thing…let's figure out what part makes you feel queasy. If the ick factor comes from you just not liking people enough to want to talk to everyone you know, everyone you meet, and everyone you get connected to, all the time, then I applaud you for being honest with yourself. I'm going to be honest with you: you probably won't build a seven-figure income, unless you're one of those magical unicorns (and

I'm really sorry you're not on our team). But maybe, just maybe, after you stick with me through the next few chapters, I can help you fall in love with talking to people. Maybe we can transform you into someone who gets all energized and lit up by interacting with other humans, and connecting them with products and a business that can enhance or even change their lives.

Maybe you're having feelings of dread because you're so unsure of what to say to people that the thought of having to struggle through that many conversations seems like a never-ending session of Chinese water torture, or worse. That's not a problem, truly, because I'm going to teach you how to talk to people in a compelling, authentic, and organic way.

Does the thought of talking to thousands exhaust you? As in, "How can I ever talk to that many people? That's like building the Golden Gate Bridge or carving Mt. Rushmore!" This doesn't worry me either, because once you get the hang of this, you'll be talking all the time and having fun doing it.

Like you, I started out as a party of one. Then I started talking to people and finding those who wanted to use the products and those who wanted to come play with me. Then I taught those folks how to do the same thing—add customers and team members—and the crazy duplication started to happen.

I'm not going to sugarcoat it. When I first started reaching out to people about my new business, I sucked. I talked too much, asked too few questions, listened too little, and spewed off too many facts. I even had someone critique me after my monologue, "Um, next time you might want to take a breath and ask a question or two, so you know if the person you're talking to is actually there."

Here's the great news. Even though I was horrible and didn't know what I was doing, I started to build a team and a customer base. In fact, the first person I ever reached out to joined me in business less than a week later and has become one of our MVPs and one of the top leaders in our entire company. Thank you, Nicole Cormany!

Reach-Out Rules to Live By

You likely have scripts and talking points from your company's training department and from your upline coaches. And they're probably really good. Yet I have a feeling that they're probably focused on facts. What I started to learn as I got more comfortable talking to people is how much more effective I could be in conversations, not by pummeling them with facts, but by following some simple, iron-clad rules. When you follow these rules you will connect authentically and emotionally with people, and find it much easier to have conversations that resonate with your prospects. You'll also find the process more purposeful and efficient. So here they are.

Reach-Out Rules

Rule #1:   Don't be attached to the outcome of any one conversation.
Rule #2:   Don't be on the hunt.
Rule #3:   Less is more.
Rule #4:   Be authentic.
Rule #5:   You can't say the wrong thing to the right person.
Rule #6:   If you find yourself convincing, stop it.
Rule #7:   Listen. Really Listen.
Rule #8:   Work from appointment to appointment.
Rule #9:   Don't count your chickens.
Rule #10:   Lead with the business, default to the products.
Rule #11:   Don't leave rambling voicemails.
Rule #12:   Lead with What's In It For Them (WIIFT).
Rule #13:   If it's a No to the business, ask for referrals.
Rule #14:   Don't end the conversation without talking about becoming your customer.

Rule #1: Don't be attached to the outcome of any one conversation.

Our job is to talk to people all the time, constantly introducing people to our business and products or services. Our job is also to get a lot of No's because this, friends, really is a numbers game. If you allow the No's to disappoint you, it will slow you down. If you allow the Maybe's to give you false hope, it will slow you down. You can't let any one conversation or any one person slow you down or distract you from your goals.

Rule #2: Don't be on the hunt.

This one may sound counterintuitive, but it's essential to the success of your business and to having authentic conversations. If your intention is "Who am I going to get today?" then I'm quite certain you'll be more focused on your own agenda than on listening to the people you talk to. You'll also run the risk of coming across pushy or—gasp—desperate.

Instead, adopt an intention of "I have something special to share, and I'm looking for people who want what I have to offer." It's not just a gimmick when we say we're not *sales*-people but *share*people. Sharing is really what we do, all over the place. As sharepeople, we don't focus on what we can get from others. Instead, we're curious about others' lives, hopes, and desires, and genuinely interested in giving—giving information, giving solutions, and if it's a good fit, giving mentoring. If someone doesn't want it, then there's no disappointment, because you weren't after anything in the first place. And this will help you with Rule #1—not being attached to the outcome of any one conversation.

In our profession our job is not to get what we want, it's to help other people get what they want. This applies to our customers and our team members. The success you're seeking will happen when you help a lot of people get what they want.

Rule #3: Less is more.

In our conversations, less is more. It's like dating. When you start seeing someone, you don't want to show too much skin right away. You don't want to be a slut. It's the same when we have conversations about our business. You don't want to be a prospecting slut.

Don't fall into the trap of thinking that if you tell your prospect everything you know about your business and your products or services, that she'll be wowed by your command of the subject and be convinced that what you're sharing is the greatest thing since the invention of Spanx. You run the risk of overwhelming or boring her, or even worse. So please, no verbal vomit.

> **You don't want to be a prospecting slut.**

Think instead about whetting your prospect's appetite. Tell them enough relevant information about the business and the products to simply get them to take a closer look, to get them to the next step. To get them to want the next date.

When you're having conversations ask yourself, "Am I talking too much? Am I being a prospecting slut right now?"

Rule #4: Be authentic.

Don't try and sound like me or anybody else. Your power—everyone's power—comes from being authentically you. People respond to people who are real. You're simply a human being who has something to offer. All you're trying to figure out is if any of those things are of value to the human being you're talking to.

When I think about all the incredibly successful leaders in our company, they're all unique...uniquely themselves.

> Be you. Be a prepared, confident you. That's where your power lies.

They're not trying to be or sound like anyone else. They let their personalities come through in conversations, presentations, and on social media. And their networks respond to them because they know it's not BS.

Be you. Be a prepared, confident you. That's where your power lies.

Rule #5: You can't say the wrong thing to the right person.

The fact that Nicole joined me in business after that pathetic first attempt to explain what I was doing, how great these products are, and what I thought it was going to do for me, proves this rule. Unbridled enthusiasm can go a long way, which is one of the reasons why you want to talk live to people instead of hiding behind emails, texts, or direct messages. Don't let the fear of not saying everything perfectly keep you from reaching out. I love what Tony Robbins has to say about being perfect, "Perfection is the absolute lowest standard you can have for yourself because it's impossible to attain."

This quest for perfection leads to a chicken and egg problem: you can't get better if you don't talk to people, but you're afraid to talk to people because you're not good enough. While you're running around in circles in your head, someone else will reach out to the people on your list and acquire them as customers or business partners. If someone is looking for what you have to offer, and it's the right time for them, they'll bite. It turned out that Nicole's employer was having issues paying his employees, so she was looking for a flexible, part-time gig that she could work around her two daughters. She wasn't finding much, and then I called.

Rule #6: If you find yourself convincing, stop it.

Avoid going into "convincing mode" because it's unproductive at best, and a total turn-off at worst. I frequently hear business builders lament, "I need to convince (insert prospect name) to jump in." I learned early on in my business that \ e don't want to convince anyone of anything.

How do you know if you're in convincing mode, you wonder? If it feels like you're trying to drag your prospect to a purchase or enrollment, you're in convincing mode. I promise you, it won't end well. Dragging people to make a decision in our favor ends up slowing us down and gives that poor person rug burn. It makes them want to run for the hills in the other direction. And if they actually purchase from us or join our team, they won't want to be there, because it wasn't really their decision.

If you find yourself in convincing mode, you're likely not asking the right questions to connect them with what this really could do for them. Or they're just not ready.

> Dragging people to make a decision in our favor ends up slowing us down and gives that poor person rug burn.

Rule #7: Listen. Really Listen.

As important as it is to talk to people with the right posture, tone, to hit the right points, and tell a compelling story, it's equally important to listen. Because you can only learn about who they are, what they want and what they fear when you give them room to talk, and you really listen. The more you know about your prospect, the more you can show them why what you have to offer fits what they're looking for.

Rule #8: Work from appointment to appointment.

When our team members complain that they feel like they're chasing their prospects once they've started conversations with them, there's always one cause. They're not setting up the next conversation appointment while they're talking to their prospect. Sometimes it's because they simply forget to do this important step. Or they're afraid of being "pushy."

Being professional is never pushy. Your time is valuable and so is your prospect's. So as soon as a prospect enters your funnel, work from appointment to appointment, and usually no more than 24-48 hours apart, as you guide her through the process of determining how she'll fit into your business now—as a team member, a customer, and/or a referral source. Setting the next appointment during your current touch point will make for a much more efficient and enjoyable process for both you and your prospect.

Rule #9: Don't count your chickens.

It's compelling to want to put a tally mark in the win column before a team member actually enrolls or a customer makes a purchase. But don't do it! I know from experience, many experiences, that they ain't in until they're in. If you prematurely count that chicken, you'll slow down your prospecting.

Rule #10: Lead with the business, default to the products.

It's simply much more effective to lead with a business discussion, pivot to referrals and then to your products or service. It may be more comfortable for you to lead with your products or service, but you run the risk of backing yourself into a corner. If someone is not interested in trying your products or service, how the hell can you then say to them, "You're not interested in what our company sells, but you should take a look at starting a business that revolves around the very thing you're disinterested in"? You can't.

Rule #11: Don't leave rambling voicemails.

It's likely you'll get lots of voicemails when you initially reach out to people in your network without a pre-arranged time to talk. I beg you not to make the rookie mistake of leaving a long, rambling message filled with info about your exciting biz that you erroneously think will entice the person to call you back. Be brief, be breezy, and make sure to let them know you'll be calling them back if you don't hear from them first.

"Hey Jane, it's Romi. Sorry I missed you, but I'd love to pick your brain about something. I'm available to chat tonight at XX or tomorrow morning at XX. Give me a call. If I don't hear from you, I'll give you a jingle tomorrow. Thanks! Talk soon!"

You want to pick their brain, here's when you're available, and you'll call them again. Bam.

Rule #12: Lead with What's In It For Them (WIIFT).

Many business builders, including me when I started, begin conversations with prospects by launching right into what you're doing with Company X, and the facts, figures, and virtues of the company and its products or services. But I soon learned that's not the best way to immediately connect emotionally with the people we're talking to.

As I honed my prospecting skills, I saw how people would become more attentive and engaged in the conversation when I started connecting the dots between what I had to offer and what it could do for them. So I started leading my conversations with What's In It For Them (WIIFT) and how people just like them were building a business like this. With this approach the people I was talking to were more present and invested in what I was saying from the get-go. The conversations were also more efficient, natural, and more interactive. They were true conversations, instead of monologues. And my closing rate went up. I was onto something.

Then I started coaching our personal team members on this, and they reported the same thing. Then I introduced it to our team. Our peeps reported not only more success with this approach, but they were enjoying the conversations more. And if we're having fun, we're going to want to do more. So the number of reachouts increased, which led to more customers and more business partners.

So let's talk about how to lead with WIIFT. It starts with a simple exercise I do before I reach out to someone. I figure out a person's pain points and how our business can reduce or eliminate her pain. It's that simple. It only adds about two minutes to your prep work, but it's so worth it.

> **Figure out a person's pain points and how our business can reduce or eliminate her pain.**

Here's how it works. Take a piece of paper and draw a line down the middle to make two columns. On the top of the left-hand column write "PAIN"; on the right "NO PAIN." Then think about all the possible pain points in her life and how our business could provide relief. From there you'll be able to craft your opening talking points for your conversation.

Let's explore what the lists could look like for a couple of different types of people. Let's say you want to reach out to your friend Jane who's a stay at home mom who used to be a high-powered corporate chick. Maybe she's mentioned her pain points to you: she misses grown-up time, and that her head is turning to mush. She hates having to ask her husband before she spends money on herself, or perhaps the family finances are really smarting with just one paycheck. She feels like she lost a piece of herself when she left her career.

Now let's talk about how your business could reduce her pain. It could give her the ability to still be the hands-on mom that's she's been, while also making it possible for her to build something of her very own. The business could help her create an extra stream of income that she might need, whether it's to pay for all the kids' activities or her shameless shoe fund. Plus, ours is a super fun business that can provide a much-needed grown-up social outlet.

So this is what her lists might look like:

PAIN	NO PAIN
• Misses making her own money	• Bring in an income
• Misses time with grown-ups	• Social/collaborative business
• Misses identity outside of wife/mom	• Can have it all hands-on mom

So how do you take the golden nuggets on these lists and turn that into an authentic and compelling conversation opener when she answers the phone?

How about something like this, "Hey, Jane, it's Romi. You've been on my mind a lot lately. Do you have a few minutes for me to pick your brain about something? I need about five minutes. Is this a good time?"

If she says it's not a good time, then you book another time. You say, "No problem. Let's work around your schedule. I'll give you a shout tonight. Which works better—eight or nine?"

But if she says, "Sure, what's up?" you lead with WIIFT.

"I've been thinking of you a lot because I remember us talking about how you love being there for the kids, but you really miss having something of your own for your sanity, your identity and your bank account. I thought of you because I'm now working with so many women just like you who are spending part-time hours every week building lucrative businesses of their very own, while still being hands on moms with flexible schedules. They're able to pay for their kids' activities, fill college and vacation funds, and even in some cases, replace income from big old corporate careers like the one you had."

"I have no idea if this would be a good fit for you, but it might be a way for you to have your cake and eat it too. I'd love to tell you what I'm up to."

Do you see how it was all about her? If you're Jane and that is your life and I've pointed out to you what some of your pain is and how I could alleviate it, don't you think that the least you would say is, "OK, I'm curious. Tell me what you're doing?"

Then, from there, you would continue with some short introductory message points about your company, and then transition to your personal story and key attributes of your business and products or service. And then, "So Jane, are you intrigued enough to want to learn more and see if this might be a good fit for you?"

Notice my posture and language made it clear that I'm really not attached to the outcome, whether or not Jane says Yes or No. I'm just sharing and helping Jane figure out if this might be a good fit for her.

Let's do another example of the Pain/No Pain analysis and intro, so you get the hang of this.

Let's say you know someone, let's call her Dana, who's a lawyer and a mom who is undeniably on a hamster wheel. You've seen her rushing to her kids' sporting events, often getting there late, looking harried and tired. You don't know her very well. You're acquaintances. But you can make educated guesses about her pain.

She wants more flexibility. She's exhausted. She might spend time thinking about how she could possibly escape from the corporate grind, but can't figure out how to make it happen when her family needs her lawyer income.

Her lists:

PAIN	NO PAIN
• Tired of the impossible schedule	• Wants flexibility for her family
• Needs the big lawyer income	• Can grow a replacement income
• Doesn't love the pressure at work	• Add more fun to her life

The conversation opener would be something like, "Dana, I see what you do. You're a superwoman with your big job and your kids. I wanted to tell you about my business because I work with so many working moms like you, who are juggling kids and their demanding jobs. They're building side businesses that are growing big enough to give them more choices, including being able to leave the corporate grind. I'd love to tell you what I'm up to. Even if it's not for you, I have a feeling you're going to know some people that I could help."

Once you get the hang of this approach, you can do it for anyone you want to reach out to—nurses, teachers, real estate professionals, you name it. But you may be wondering how to use this approach if you haven't talked to the person in a long time or don't know someone well. If you're Facebook friends, you can glean a lot of information from her posts. Here's a real life example of how I helped a team member do a little sleuthing to figure out potential pain points.

Our team member Julie wanted to reach out to her sorority sister Lynn who lives in Louisville. She hadn't talked to Lynn in more than a decade, and didn't know what to say to her. I asked her what she did know about Lynn. "I can tell she's got a real successful career now in finance or accounting or something with money. And she always had the best personality and was a real go getter."

I told Julie that I bet she knows more than that about Lynn through her Facebook posts. We scrolled through Lynn's wall and were able to confirm that she likes to travel and she's into the nicer things in life, having posted about killer shoes and sporting some gorgeous jewelry in her pictures. We also learned she has a high schooler who might be going to college in a few years. While we didn't know for sure what Lynn's pain was, we were able to create the lists to give Julie some good introductory message points.

PAIN	NO PAIN
• Expensive tastes	• More income
• Kid going to college soon	• Fill college funds

It's not much, but it's all Julie needed to get ready to reach out. Since Julie didn't have Lynn's phone number, she reached out through Facebook messaging in an attempt to set up a call.

"Lynn, we haven't talked in ages, but I love keeping up with you through your posts. I'm thrilled to see that life has been so good to you. I'd love to pick your brain for my business since I have a feeling you might know some people in Louisville that I could help. I work with lots of women who love earning extra money for travel funds, shameless shoe funds, or even to pay for college. I know your son will be there real soon, so you might even want to learn more for yourself. I'd love to set up a time to chat for ten minutes...Well, better make it 20 so we can really catch up properly. I'm available tomorrow night at eight or 8:30 or Thursday at noon. Tell me which one works and the best number to reach you."

Notice that I coached Julie to give Lynn times when she likely wouldn't be engulfed in her corporate day job, so Julie offered two evening times and one during a possible lunch break.

Lynn responded to Julie that day. They had a terrific conversation, and Julie was able to make it really clear what could be in it for Lynn. Lynn wasn't personally interested since she loved her lucrative job, and her inheritance provided more than enough for her family. But she connected Julie with a friend of hers with a similar taste for the finer things and two kids in high school, who ended up joining her team. And Lynn became a customer.

Even if you're not able to sleuth out what someone's life looks like now, you can rely on what you know about that person from the past. I hadn't talked to my childhood friend Shelley for years. Yet I vividly remembered her ambition was apparent even at a young age. How she went after what she wanted and made things happen. She also had a magnetic personality. People just loved being around her.

Even though I didn't have pain points, I reached out to Shelley leading with how I'm working with people that remind me of her. I didn't have her phone number, so I messaged her on Facebook.

"Shelley, I know we haven't talked live in ages, but I've been thinking about you a lot lately since I'm working with people who remind me so much of you. I'd love to pick your brain for my business. You've always been someone who is so driven and gets things done, and you've got a magnetic personality. These are things I look for in my business. I have no idea if what I do will be a good fit for you. But if it is, you can have a heck of a lot of fun spending part time hours building something pretty substantial. And if it's not, I have a feeling you'll know some other dynamic go-getters who might be a good fit. When can you hop on the phone for five to ten minutes so I can fill you in? I'm free tonight after eight or tomorrow at noon."

Shelley responded, telling me she was intrigued to learn more and to catch up. When she and I talked, I learned about her pain points and was able to explain how this business could reduce her pain of long hours at her stressful job and not enough extra money to splurge on herself. She ultimately joined our team.

Remember, if you simply can't figure out someone's pain, and all you have to go on is their profession or that they're a mother, or a woman, don't worry about it. You can always say, "I know so many people just like you who have been successful doing what I do, so I thought you'd want to take a look and decide if this might be a good fit for you, too." Since I have no doubt there are people in your company just like them, this is an authentic statement!

Get in Action

Now it's your turn. Take out a piece of paper and draw a line down the middle to make two columns. On the top of the left-hand column write "PAIN"; on the right "NO PAIN." Then think of the next person you want to reach out to. List all the possible pain points in her life and how our business could provide relief. From there you'll be able to craft your opening talking points for your conversation. Do this exercise every time before you reach out to someone, and you'll be leading with WIIFT.

Rule #13: If it's a No to the business, ask for referrals.

If someone isn't personally interested in the business, make sure to immediately pivot to a request for referrals. Simply say, "I totally get that this is not for you, Maggie. It's not for everyone. But I'd love to pick your brain about your network, since I have a feeling you likely know some people I could help. Do you have a couple more minutes so I can describe exactly who I'm looking for and we'll see whose names pop into your head?"

Notice a couple things: 1) I asked for permission to continue, which is not only good manners, but also continues the interactivity of the conversation; and 2) I've planted the seed that names are going to pop into her head.

When asking for referrals, I've had much more success when I'm specific about who I'm looking for. I used to be so vague in my request for connections, asking who they knew who had big personalities, or were go-getters or real dynamos. I rarely was given any names.

> When asking for referrals, I've had much more success when I'm specific about who I'm looking for.

But I started getting referrals when I got real specific about who I was looking for. I focused on certain demographics so it was easier for people to think of who they knew who fit the description.

So here's what I always say now. "Here's what I'm looking for," I begin, and then the first demographic I describe is always someone just like the person I'm talking to. This is because I want her to hear again how someone just like her does well in this business.

If I'm talking to a teacher I say, "I really love working with teachers because they're so good at being coachable and teaching others to do this really simple business. Teachers love making more money because they're underpaid, and they love having the option down the road to spend more time with their own kids rather than other people's. Plus this business is great insulation from the pink slip."

Then I cover the other demographics that I'm always looking for. "I also absolutely love working with stay at home moms who need flexibility with their kids, but really need an extra stream of income. It's possible to grow a lucrative business while still being a hands-on mom."

I also always describe the corporate mom that's tied to the hamster wheel. Then because of John's and my success, and the success of many others on our team, I add in a request for couples who are entrepreneurial, successful, and might want to add another smart business to their professional portfolio.

"I get to work with a number of couples who together, each working just part time hours every week, are able to build these incomes that are fully funding college funds or retirement funds, and just opening up a whole wealth of possibilities for them."

If somebody doesn't come up with specific referrals for me right on the phone, I will simply say to them, "It might be hard for you to think of people right now. Would it be helpful if I sent you a brief email summarizing what we talked about and exactly who I'm looking for? You'll be able to easily forward it to anybody you think of and copy me on it. Does that sound good?"

I've been connected with loads of referrals this way. In the email, I not only briefly summarize what our business is, but I also include a bulleted list of the demographics I'm looking for. And guess who I describe in the very first bullet? The person I'm writing to, of course, so she can be reminded that people just like her are building our business—to entice her to think about it for herself.

When people offer referrals, make sure to ask a couple questions about the person they're connecting you with, so you can identify her pain points and prepare a compelling conversation opener.

Rule #14: Don't end the conversation without talking about becoming your customer.

Whatever you do, don't let go of that person without segueing to the products. You'll develop your own easy transition to a product or service discussion. If you're representing nutritional products, maybe your transition question is, "If you could have more energy to do the things you want to do, would that make a difference in your life?" Because I work in skincare, I've always transitioned by asking, "Before I let you go, I've got to ask you, if you could change one thing about your skin, what would it be?"

> Whatever you do, don't let go of that person without segueing to the products.

To date, I have only had one person say, "Nothing. I am absolutely in love with my face." It turned out that she has had every plastic surgery and outpatient procedure known to man. I don't think the woman's face moves. Everyone else, however, offers up a complaint. And guess what? I've got the solution for what they're bitching about. So find your transition question that works for you and your products, and ask it every single time.

If you're unable to close the sale during that conversation, remember Rule #8 and set up the next appointment within 24-48 hours to get their questions answered and take their order. Never—I repeat—never let them make their own purchase. People will invariably forget or do it wrong, or opt out of the autoship program if your company has one. Instead walk them through the purchase process. It's not only great customer service, but it also ensures you actually acquire the customer in the right way.

Wash. Rinse. Repeat.

These are the initial conversations you'll have with people. Lots and lots of people. You'll get really good at it the more conversations you have. You'll get more comfortable and more authentic. You'll become a better listener and learn how to make a compelling case for WIIFT. You won't be a prospecting slut. And you'll have fun. I promise.

But having thousands of introductory conversations alone won't get you to a seven-figure income. You have to guide someone who's intrigued enough to want to learn more through the decision-making process. Wanna know how? Let me guide you to the next step. You can turn the page now or tomorrow at 10:30. Which one works for you?

CHAPTER 6

She's Interested...
Now What?

First, I want you to know that I've come to dislike the traditional sales term "close." Because I think it promotes hunter behavior. Instead, I like to think of the next stage of the conversation as the decision-making process, and your role is to help your prospect to determine if your business or your products are a good fit for her at this time. It involves getting someone through your funnel as quickly and efficiently as possible, to find out how they fit into your business right now—as a team member, a customer, a connector, or a "not right now." Because as you'll learn, if you haven't already, there's nothing worse than a constipated funnel!

During this process, you want to stay focused on the Rules from the last chapter, because they all still apply. Above all, your job while you take a prospect through their decision is to guide them through the exploratory process, and help them figure out if you have something of use for them. Everything you say and do should be motivated by helping someone come to the right decision for them. Remember, you aren't attached to the outcome of any one conversation. If you keep the process this simple, you'll be more confident and purposeful, and a lot more efficient.

> Everything you say and do should be motivated by helping someone come to the right decision for them.

In *Blink*, Malcom Gladwell talks about two types of decision makers—the "gunslingers" and the methodical, analytical, need-to-look-at-things-from-every-angle-and-all-sides-type. The key to effective and efficient closing practices is to keep control of the process and the   regardless of what type of decision-maker you're talking to.

According to Gladwell, great decision makers aren't those who process the most information or spend the most time deliberating, but those who have perfected the art of "thin-slicing," filtering the few factors that matter from an overwhelming number of variables.

The closing tools that successful business builders use are designed to help people, regardless of the type of decision maker, in their thin-slicing. We want to help each person filter the factors important to their decision-making, so they're able to come to a quicker decision that's right for them.

It's been my experience that gunslingers are more rare. It's interesting to note that in our entire huge organization, almost every single one of the most successful business builders have been gunslingers with regard to making the decision whether to start a business. Even if they said No first, they said No quickly. And when they took another look, they said Yes quickly.

I'm certainly not suggesting that you should write off anyone who doesn't come to a quick decision. But your process should be designed to add the gunslingers as quickly as possible, show them how to do the same, and help the rest come to a decision that serves them and doesn't slow *you* down in the process.

When you're talking to a prospect and you've led with WIIFT, shared a brief overview about your company and your products or services, and told your short personal story, a simple way to move the conversation forward is to ask, "So, are you intrigued enough to want to learn more?" or

"Would you like to learn more to see if this might be a good fit for you?"

If they answer affirmatively, tell them you'll be sending them a few things to look over and/or listen to. What those things are will depend on what your company and your up-line leaders provide for you to use in your closing process. It may include videos, recorded calls, website content, blogs, and more. But remember Rule #3—Less is More. Don't overwhelm your prospect with too much content. I coach our team to send a brief and compelling video of our founders, a short info call I recorded, and an entry or two from our company's blog that they think will resonate with their prospect.

Then it's essential to tee up the next conversation. If there's an event in the next 24-48 hours, invite her to that.

"After reviewing everything, I know you'll have some questions. We're having a get-together tomorrow night. It would be the perfect opportunity to get your questions answered, get a sense of how collaborative this business is, and figure out if you'd like to be a part of it. I'd love to put you on the guest list."

It's important to understand why I'm putting a time limit on the next event of just 24-48 hours. If the event is farther away, why wait to push the prospect through your funnel? You can set up a three-way conference call instead, and actually use the upcoming event as a closing carrot for coming in during that conversation. "If this is a good fit, you should really get started and take advantage of our event next week to start growing your team and customer base." Remember that we want to move our prospects through the process as quickly as possible. The more time they have between touch points, the more likely

> **We want to move our prospects through the process as quickly as possible.**

it is that they'll get cold feet or talk to someone with a poor opinion of our profession.

If there isn't an event right around the corner, or if your prospect can't make the event, then tee up the conference call. "After reviewing everything, I know you'll have some questions. So let's schedule a time to talk so we can get them all answered. I'm going to invite my friend and business partner to join us. She'll give you another perspective, and together we can help you figure out if this is a good fit for you."

It's helpful to have pre-arranged times when your upline is available or access to your upline's calendar of available slots through an online calendaring service. If you don't have either, simply get three available times the prospect will be available in the next, you guessed it, 24-48 hours, and then loop with your upline to determine which one works.

If you're freaked out or nervous about offering a conference call with your upline, get over it. It's one of the most important closing tools we have in our tool kit. We'll thoroughly explore how to execute three-way calls in this chapter. Just remember to position the call as a resource to help your prospect, which is exactly what it is.

Throughout this conversation, your prospect might start asking questions. Answer the ones you feel comfortable answering. The simple answers to common objections in the next chapter will help, but by no means think that you're supposed to have an exhaustive conversation at this point. Remember, your job is to guide them to the next step. The next step is to take a look at or listen to more information, and to either hop on a call with a biz partner or go to an event.

Here's the key: don't ask, but **tell** your prospect what the next steps are. Your prospect isn't in the business. She doesn't know how it works or the most efficient way to explore whether it's a good fit. You're the expert. Speak with confidence. Don't ask the prospect if they want to have a conversation with your biz partner. Tell her the next step to help her decide is a phone conversation with you and your biz partner, because she should get another team member's perspective, and you know she'll have questions. If you remember the difference, it will change the speed of your prospect's decision.

Especially when you're green, it's helpful to have what I like to call a "pivot statement" to stop the seemingly, never-ending stream of questions that occasionally happen, and move the prospect to the next step. Simply say, "These are great questions, and it definitely sounds like you want more info. So let me tell you what we'll do next." Then go through the process above of teeing up the next steps. Easy peasy.

> Here's the key: don't ask, but *tell* your prospect what the next steps are.

Three-way, anyone?

We've talked about how to introduce the three-way call to your prospects. Now we are going to focus on how to effectively execute this mother of decision-making tools. Believe in the three-way. Crave the three-way. Master the three-way.

I must point out that even though we refer to these calls as three-ways and greatly delight in the sexual innuendo, don't use this term in the outside world. Instead, call them "a phone chat" or "a conversation,"

First, let's cover why you should believe in them:

* They provide compelling third-party legitimization
* They allow your upline to train you how to handle objections and bring a prospect to a close
* They move your prospect through your funnel efficiently

* Even if you can bring your prospects quickly to a decision on your own, the majority of your team members likely won't be able to.

> **Believe in the three-way.**
> **Crave the three-way.**
> **Master the three-way.**

Now the logistics. If there's been a day or more since your last conversation, it's good to confirm the call time with your prospect the day before the call via text or email. When it's time for the call, get your prospect on the phone first, then conference in your upline. To avoid those awkward technology fails, if you're not familiar with the conference-call feature on your phone, you'll want to practice it first.

For a three-way call to be successful, your upline business partner needs to be prepared with information on your prospect. Whenever possible, send your biz partner a brief email or text, whichever they prefer, the night before or at least an hour before the call. This will help your upline gather her thoughts and any stories she thinks might be helpful. Keep in mind that as you and your team members get more experienced with three-ways, you should be able to do a killer call even without prior knowledge of the prospect. This exercise also helps you properly introduce the prospect to your upline. The information should include:

* Prospect's name
* Where she lives: city, province/state, country
* How you know her
* What does she currently do professionally (or in the past)
* Why you think she would be good at this business
* What's attracting her to the business
* Whether she's driven and hardworking
* Other strengths she has
* What concerns or objections has she already raised

You and your upline must come to a three-way call with clear goals. With each call you're aiming to do one of the following: 1) enroll a new business partner; 2) book a follow-up appointment; 3) ask for referrals and enroll them as a customer.

The Flow of the Call

With those goals in mind, let's go over the flow of the call. Once everyone is on the line, introduce your prospect and your upline to each other. This short introduction should be no more than a minute. It should contain:

* An introduction
* How you know each other
* Why you think she'd be great at this
* What's in it for her

We're going to pretend now that I'm your upline sponsor and you're bringing the prospect to a three-way call with me. Here's what your introduction would sound like:

"Romi, I wanted to introduce you to my friend Jane. (Then include how you know Jane and an authentic compliment). Jane and I used to work together at a hospital in Chicago and she's one of the most outgoing and magnetic people I know. She's open to the idea of earning some extra money, but said she doesn't want to bite off more than she can chew. So I'm really excited for her to learn more about our company and how this could fit into her life." This is where you briefly add in specifics that reiterate why you want to work with your prospect—demonstrating that you really listened to her, and letting her hear WIIFT once again.

"Jane, I'm thrilled you get the chance to talk with my friend, Romi. She'll give you her perspective and answer any questions you have. Romi, I'll let you take it from here."

Once you finish the introduction, you stop talking. I take it from there and run the call, and you don't talk unless I ask you to chime in, or unless your prospect asks you something directly. It's important for me as the upline to quickly set the tone of the call at the beginning, taking the pressure off the prospect so they're more open to hearing what I have to say.

"I remember being in your shoes, Jane, and I wasn't sure what to expect on a call like this. But I want you to know that I'm not in the business of trying to convince anyone that they should start a business of their own. It's simply my job to share my experience and answer any questions you may have to see if this is a good fit for you. Does that sound good?"

> It's important for me as the upline to quickly set the tone of the call at the beginning, taking the pressure off the prospect so they're more open to hearing what I have to say.

Then I share my short story, making sure to highlight any common points that are relevant and relatable to her. Then I ask her why she's intrigued about our business, which draws out her WHY. Her answer will help me tailor my answers to her upcoming questions, and to replay them back to her when I ask her to make a decision.

Then I briefly share the facts of our business, emphasis on **briefly**. I specifically use the word "facts," because at this point in the conversation I'm not sharing opinions. I'm listing the inarguable facts about our company, our products, the business channel, and the income potential in succinct and compelling message points.

Next, I turn the conversation back to the prospect. *"I've shared a lot of information, Jane. What questions do you have?"* This is almost always the longest part of the call in which I answer Jane's questions about what we do, how we do it, and how she could do it too. And I field her objections.

Once all the questions have been answered and the objections addressed, it's time to gauge the prospect's readiness to make a decision.

"Ok Jane, tell me, on a scale of 1 to 10—1 you are ready to hang up the phone and run, and 10 that you'd like to get started today, where are you?"

If she says 1 to 4, I'd respond, *"This business doesn't seem like it's a good fit for you,"* and immediately move to a conversation about becoming a customer and getting referrals.

If she says 6 or 7, I'd move the business conversation forward. *"It seems like you still have some questions to get you more comfortable. What can I help answer?"* This will get to the core objection(s).

If she's an 8 or 9, I know I'm likely to help her decide to join our business on the call. So I show Jane what the next step is. If she's ready to enroll, I describe the simple way we'll get her started and ask if she has a few minutes now. If she doesn't have time then, I prompt you and Jane to schedule a time right then for later today or tomorrow for an enrollment appointment.

As we've all experienced, immediate enrollment doesn't always happen (wouldn't that be **nice**), even if a prospect is a 9 or 10. Quite often they need to discuss it with their husbands, check their finances, get through busy projects at their day jobs, etc. So you want to be ready to respond with next steps that will keep her moving through the funnel, and will help you and your team member maintain control of the timeline.

If the prospect needs to talk with her husband, validate that. *"Of course you should discuss this with your husband. Let me know if he has any questions. I talk to husbands all the time. Can you talk with him tonight?"* Then book a follow-up appointment right then, inviting the husband as well, for no later than 48 hours. It's been my experience that if you wait any longer than that, you'll likely lose them. If your team has access to an info call specifically tailored for husbands—my husband John has a phenomenal one for our team that speaks to the specific questions spouses have—mention it to your prospect, and send it immediately following the call.

If they aren't interested in the business, enroll them as a customer. *"I totally understand if this business isn't for you. It isn't for everyone. But these products (or services) are for everyone. I'd be honored to have you as my customer."*

Remember to ask for referrals. By now, you know the drill, *"You may know some people who I can help. Here's who I'm looking for* (include detailed descriptions and always describe the person you're talking to first)."

Remember, whether you're bringing the call to your upline, or the upline is leading the call, be confident and know that you're providing a helpful and efficient forum for the prospect to decide if she wants to join you in business, start benefitting from your products or services, or connect you with people in her network.

There are three reasons why three-ways go bad.

1) **The call runs too long.**

   Calls are usually no more than 15-25 minutes, max. This is for several reasons.

   * You don't want to overwhelm the prospect.
   * It's not duplicable for busy working people to have 30-45 minute calls throughout the day to work their biz.
   * It's not possible for busy leaders to fit in that many calls in a week, if they're all marathon gabfests.
   * Generally speaking, everything that needs to be said can be accomplished in that time. If you're going over 15-20

minutes, you're being redundant and not focusing on the things you should be—which are handling objections and guiding the prospect to a decision.

Now of course there are exceptions to the brevity rule. For example, if you've got a talker on the line who just won't shut up, make sure they feel they're being "heard," but guide the conversation as quickly as you can to the important parts.

> **If you're going over 15-20 minutes, you're being redundant and not focusing on the things you should be.**

You'll also have calls with prospects who have a gazillion questions, since they're trying to explore and understand every single aspect of the business. Listen to and answer all her questions, but it you run out of time, don't hesitate to schedule a follow-up call later in the day or tomorrow, and have your business partner send relevant information that addresses some of her outstanding questions. Yet make sure that you're not in convincing mode. If you find yourself convincing someone to do this, the call's gone on too long.

I always let my business partners know either before the call, or before adding in the prospect, how much time I have and to keep an eye on the clock. It's her job to keep an eye on the time and make sure that she's helping you get off the phone. I train my team members to simply say, during a pause in the conversation, "I know you've got to go, Romi, so why don't you take one more question, and then we can always schedule a time to continue the conversation later today."

2) **Your business partner doesn't set up the call correctly.**
   It's imperative that you teach your team how to intro the call once all the parties are there. The introductions are the key to kicking off the call with a casual and relaxed vibe. It's

so awkward for all three people when the builder bringing her prospect doesn't launch into introductions, instead allowing awkward silence.

3) **Your upline doesn't fact find at the beginning.**

If you don't take the time to ask the prospects about their life and why they're interested in the business, you miss out on valuable information that will help you show them why your business makes sense for them. Allow them to tell you about their life and their pain points, so you can later demonstrate that people just like them are having success. Since people love talking about themselves most, this helps build rapport between you and the prospect.

Anyone who's brought me a three-way call has heard me ask this question, "So, Prospect, my friend gave you a great intro, but I'd like to hear a bit more about you and your life, and what is it about our business that's intriguing you most?" This usually gives me enough to know what to highlight most during the rest of the call.

Guide her to a decision.

Whether you're guiding someone to a decision on a three-way call for your downline, or having a one-on-one with someone at a coffee date or after she's attended an event, there's an efficient and helpful way to naturally transition the conversation. After you've answered all her objections, replay what the prospect has told you she's looking for. This brings you full circle, right back to WIIFT.

This is why listening throughout your conversations is so important. It might sound something like this, "Jane, I think this could be a great fit for you. You want to find a way to take fewer consulting gigs so you can spend more time with your kids, and to really insulate yourself from the down markets. Since it sounds like you'd be able to squeeze this business in around everything else on your plate, you love people, and like the idea of helping other people succeed, this could work really well for you. Do you agree?"

> After you've answered all her objections, replay what the prospect has told you she's looking for.

Then you'd tell her, "Our next step is to tell you how we get you started. Sound good?"

There are times you've connected all the dots, and replayed WIIFT, but there's still hesitation. There are a few helpful arrows to have in your quiver to get her to make a decision. You may decide to use one or all of them.

* Ask where she's at on the scale. Just as I coached you to do in the three-way call, this will help you see how far away she is from a "Yes" and help you get to the root of her hesitation.

* Ask her what's at the root of her hesitation. Since you've likely answered all the typical objections that we review thoroughly in the next chapter, it's likely because of the business model or lack of belief in herself. Don't be afraid to ask and get to the bottom of it. Because remember, you can't educate about what's hidden.

If it's because of the business model, ask more questions. "Is it because you don't fully understand how it works or because you're worried what others will think?" Again, this will help you get to the root of her hesitation.

Be honest with her. "Some people might think you're crazy because you're doing this. But here's the important question—why do you care? You're the one trying to juggle your demanding job and your family, and still not feeling like you have enough money to get ahead. There will be people who don't support your business, but this decision isn't about them. It's about you and what you want."

The best way to handle lack of self-confidence is with an explanation of the support she'll get, and success stories of others just like her. I'm very honest with prospects who doubt themselves. "Ultimately you've got to be willing to believe that you deserve to have more. That I cannot give you. That's got to come from you. You've got to be willing to believe that you deserve more than (whatever their pain is)."

* Ask her about her Plan B. Replay her WHY to her once again, and then simply ask, if it's not through this business, what's her Plan B to achieve her WHY.

* Talk about the worst-case scenario. This works well to point out there is very little to lose and, at the least, some great things to gain. I usually add in some dramatic flair that lessens the enormity of the decision and elicits some giggles. "OK, Jane. Let's talk about the worst-case scenario for you. It's not like you're about to invest half a million to open a franchise. The worst thing that could happen is (list the potential benefits or your products or services) at wholesale pricing, you'll earn your investment back if you just do a little work, and you'll be eligible for tax deductions that come with a home-based business. And you might have some fun."

There's no doubt that you can master the skill of bringing people to their decision. It will become easier and more instinctual the more you do it. Please don't sabotage yourself by making up the story in your head that professional, efficient, and helpful conversations that ask your prospects to make decisions are pushy. Professional, efficient, and helpful is exactly what you and your prospects deserve. You've got a gift to share and you're looking for people who want what you have to offer. And when you do, it's a blast. It's the reason that I still wake up every single day wanting to reach out and find our next business partners.

> You've got a gift to share and you're looking for people who want what you have to offer.

CHAPTER 7

I OBJECT!

People will offer objections as to why they don't think the business is right for them. Don't fear objections, embrace them! Objections are a helpful way to move the conversation about your business forward—when you treat them like requests for more information. I LOVE objections for four reasons:

1. They invite a real conversation about the prospect, the business, and whether or not the two will be a good fit.

2. They show the prospect is actually invested enough in the conversation to ask questions. We can work with that!

3. It begins the training process. If your objecting prospect joins your team, you'll have already shown her that objections aren't an impediment to adding a team member, but simply part of the process. Plus you've already started showing her how to respond to them.

4. Educating people about this business is so much fun. The most enlightening and authentic conversations come from exploring prospects' objections. But we can't educate what's hidden.

The most important things to remember in handling objections are: don't get defensive and don't go into convincing mode! We are sorting people, not convincing them. If your focus remains on being of service to your prospect to help him or her understand our business model, your company's proposition, and WIIFT, the conversation will be relaxed, authentic, efficient, and helpful.

Here's the great news: there are only a handful of objections we all get, and once you're comfortable handling them, you can confidently help your personal prospects and those brought to you on three-way calls to make educated decisions as to whether they want to start their own business. Of course, you may get objections unique to your product or service, but I'm going to assume that between your company and your upline, you're in great hands to learn how to handle them.

When someone raises an objection, I love using the approach I learned from an industry veteran and one of the most authentic communicators I've ever known, Richard Bliss Brooke—respond with a question. A clarifying question is so helpful, because people often don't really understand what they're objecting to or they have incorrect assumptions. The answer to your clarifying question gives you more information about what your prospect is really thinking. You'll see how this plays out below.

> **People often don't really understand what they're objecting to or they have incorrect assumptions.**

While we want our prospects to feel heard and don't want to discount their feelings, it's our job to explain why their concerns shouldn't keep them from starting a business of their own. Until you get comfortable with responding to objections, an effective format for your answers (after you've asked the clarifying question) is "feel-felt-found":

*"I understand how you **feel** about _____. I've **felt** that way before, but here's what I've **found**..."*

Over time, you'll become even more authentic and natural with your responses, perhaps abandoning "feel-felt-found," which can sound trite.

So let's talk about the most common objections and how you can knock it out of the park with your answers. Each objection is followed by a suggested Clarifying Question, and then a proposed answer to use after your prospect has addressed your question.

I don't think I have enough time to do this.

Clarifying Question: *"How much time do you think you need to start building your own business?"*

"I'm actually looking for busy people, because I've learned that busy people get things done. I must tell you that I wasn't sure how I was going to fit this in, but most of us work this business in very part-time hours around everything else on our plates. It requires consistent effort of doing a little bit each day, and working it into your everyday life and conversations. And let's be honest, we can find time for the things that are a priority—whether it's building a business or watching a Game of Thrones marathon."

Dig in further to find out what your prospect would like to do with this. *"So you're telling me you'd want to build an exit strategy from your job (or whatever their why is). In 10-15 hours a week—ten minutes here, 20 minutes here, half-hour there—you can invest your time in achieving those goals. So what I'm interested in learning is not whether you think you have the time for this, but if you want to devote the time to this. Are you willing to invest that time toward (repeat their WHY)?"*

I don't have the money to do this.

Clarifying Question: *"If money wasn't an issue, would you want to jump in and build a business that could help you (repeat their WHY)?"*

"If you don't have the money to invest in a business of your own that can grow an additional income stream for you, it shows just how badly you could use this. Do you have the investment amount on a credit card? If you do, we'll teach you how to make your investment back through product sales, and growing your team (and any other incentives your company offers). *I will keep you laser-focused on the income-producing activity that will get you a return on your investment."*

If they say they need time to get the money together, then I schedule an enrollment appointment so they have a deadline to work toward. I also assign them the homework of solidifying their WHY and writing down their initial Dream Team List. When I confirm their enrollment appointment a few days prior, I request this info. The homework gives them a head start, keeps their future business top-of-mind, and it shows me how serious they are about doing this. Plus, if they ultimately don't join, I ask them to connect me with their Dream Team List they've already compiled. They can't tell you they didn't think of someone to connect you with.

I don't want to bother friends.

Clarifying Question: *"Why do you think you'd be bothering friends?"*

"I'm so glad to hear that because that's not what we do. We share about products (or a service) that we love and a business that can enhance or change lives. If you're coming across like you're bugging someone, you're not being coachable, and you're not following our simple system. We'll teach you how to casually and conversationally talk to people you know and people you're referred to. And look, not everyone will want your products or want to join your business. But that's ok."

I don't know enough people.

Clarifying Question: *"How many people do you think you need to know?"*

"We all know a lot of people. We'll help you jog your memory so you remember all the people you've met in your life. One of the many things I love about this business is that it's not necessarily who you know, but the contacts of those that you do know. Plus, this business is a great way to get to know new people. We'll teach you how. Remember, don't prejudge what someone else is looking for. You never know who's looking for exactly what you have to offer. I think you probably know enough people to start building a business. What I'm really interested in is how much you like people. Because this business is all about people. If you don't enjoy talking to people, lots of people, then you won't have fun, and you won't show up. So let's talk about how much you love people."

I'm not a salesperson.

Clarifying Question: *"Why do you think you need a sales background?"*

"I'm not looking for salespeople. I'm looking for passionate people who love to share about things they love. I'm also looking for people who enjoy helping others. Does this sound like you? If it does, we can teach you how we do what we do. And let's face it, even those of us who have never been in traditional sales, still sell. We sell ideas. Heck, I sell ideas to my kids every day to get them to do what I want them to do."

The timing just isn't right for me to start a business.

Clarifying Question: *"What would make it the right time?"*

"*The timing of starting a business, like having kids, will never be perfect. Perfect doesn't exist. But it sounds like you want to* (repeat their WHY). *Let's talk about how this could fit in around everything on your plate and help you get to* (their WHY)."

If they still say not right now, transition to referrals and to the customer discussion. If they won't bite on either, ask your prospect if you may contact them at a later date.

Is this a pyramid?

Clarifying Question: *"What do you mean by pyramid?"*

If they answer referencing a "pyramid scheme" then continue, "*Pyramid schemes are illegal. With pyramids there is no selling of product (or services). That's not what this is.*" If I think I can be a little bit of a smartass, I add with a wink, "*Is that what you're looking for?*"

If they answer with reference to "one of those things where you build a team and the team makes you money" then continue, "*If you're asking if this is the network marketing model, absolutely yes. I wouldn't be doing it if it weren't. We get to build an organization of customers and team members, and we teach others to do the same thing. Instead of just getting paid because of my efforts, I get to earn based on the success of my whole team. Unlike most jobs, where we'd never expect to earn more than our boss, it's not uncommon for someone to earn even more than the person who invited them into the business. What other questions do you have?*"

Once you've handled all their questions and objections, then say, "*Do you have any other questions or are you ready to get started?*" If your prospect doesn't offer up any more questions, but declines to get started, simply ask, "*I sense some hesitation; what's behind that?*" In their authentic answer will be the objection that they haven't shared.

Here's what I've learned in all these years about objections: whatever you're unsure of is what you will get asked about most. Don't really believe this is a brilliant business model? You'll get asked about pyramids. Not sure you've got what it takes to share about your business and products in a compelling way because you lack sales experience? Your prospects will tell you they don't think they have the right background.

> Whatever you're unsure of is what you will get asked about most.

So make sure you have sufficiently answered **your** objections, so that you have a confident and powerful posture to field whatever objections come your way.

CHAPTER 8

She's Just Not That Into You... Or Is She?

Let's talk about an epidemic condition in our business that's likely afflicting you. You've got people stuck in your funnel, and you can't, for the life of you, get them through. I want to help you tackle this problem and be able to pull those suckers through your funnel now, without pulling your hair out. Because as I've said, there's nothing worse than a constipated funnel.

When you have people stuck in your funnel, it really messes with you and your business. It's distracting, frustrating, and emotionally and energetically draining. Just like the other kind of constipation. And, as we've already discussed, it can delude you into thinking you've got peeps likely to join your team, which will prevent you from continuing to reach out to others at the volume our business requires. So we've all got to get really good at pushing people through our funnels.

Let's start with a couple golden nuggets. First, if you're truly reaching out to enough people to keep your funnel full, you won't have any attachment to the outcome of any one person. Remember what I coach—at least three to five new people a day.

Second, let go of the fear of losing what you don't have. Too often I see builders who would rather have a prospect hang out interminably in their funnel, than ask simple, pointed questions to get to why she won't make a decision.

> Let go of the fear of losing what you don't have.

They fear the prospect will walk away from the opportunity when pushed to be honest, open, and decisive.

Let's get really clear about something. If a person is hanging out there undecided about what role, if any, they want to play in your business, you have nothing to lose. But by helping them reach a decision, you save your sanity.

Third, learn The Take Away and don't be afraid to use it. This is simply taking back the offer of the business. It's done in a very casual, non-emotional way. There are many ways to phrase it, depending on the details of your conversations, but it may be as simple as, "I just don't think this is the right fit for you. It's not for everyone." Then segue into a discussion about referrals and your products or services.

If you're not starting and continuing conversations in the way I've laid out in the previous chapters, then it's no wonder people are dangling in your funnel. *They don't know what to do next.* They're not being asked to make a decision. So I implore you to really give all of that a shot, including three-way calls. Truly, this system works.

What I want to focus on now are all those other situations where prospects get stuck, despite following all the rules. Because it happens to all of us. Here's the great news: most of the time you'll find that someone is stuck simply because you're not asking enough questions. Our job is to ask enough questions and really listen to the answers so we can figure out, and sometimes help her figure out, if this is really something she wants to do or if she's just not that into you. Let's explore how this works.

> **Most of the time you'll find that someone is stuck simply because you're not asking enough questions.**

Can't get someone on a three-way call.

Your prospect Mary says she's interested, but won't commit to a three-way call and won't enroll. You've even perfectly positioned the phone chat to illustrate WIIFT, but she responds, "No, I don't think I need one right now." Has this ever happened to you? Of course it has. It happens to us all.

Instead of just saying ok, you should ask some questions.

"So you feel that you have all the information you need at this time to decide if this is a good fit for you, Mary?" If she says, "Yes" then let's wave our hands in the air and shout "whoop whoop," because it's easy to segue to a closing conversation.

"That's terrific, Mary. It sounds like you're ready to start building your own turnkey business so you can pay for all your kids' activities and have some leftover and you won't have to ask your husband permission when you want to have your spa days (or whatever you learned her reasons why might be)."

If she is, you get her enrolled. If she says No, then keep asking questions.

"So what more information do you need in order to make a decision?" If she responds with, "I don't know," then you're able to say, "This is why I think you'd get a lot out of a short call with my friend and biz partner. This is the best way for you to understand how this might work for you and if you want to be part of it. If it's ultimately not a good fit, that's ok. At least you'll know."

If she still pushes back, then keep asking questions. "I'm sensing that you're not comfortable getting on the phone with one of the people I work with. Am I right? What's that about?"

The answer will likely include not wanting to feel pressured or ganged up on, or some other assumption. Be honest and authentic and show her that you're truly not attached to the outcome.

"Look, the last thing I want to do is to convince you of anything. If this isn't something you're excited about, then you won't be a good fit. But if you're hesitating because you're nervous about whether you could actually build this and how it might fit into your life, those are all questions we can explore together. It's natural to be nervous. We all are, since this is out of our comfort zones. This call is simply an opportunity for you to further explore if this is the vehicle that can get you to where you tell me you want to be."

If she still doesn't want to move the process forward with a three-way call, guess what? She's not into you! Let's be real. If she's not open to a damn conference call to further discuss a business proposition, is she going to be any good at our business? Hell to the no. So don't leave people like Mary dangling in your funnel. Push them through and move on to the next person. Because that's how you grow your business.

"You know, Mary, I really sense that this isn't a good fit for you, at least right now. So now that you've got a good idea what this is about, let's talk about who you know who just might want to start a part-time biz of their own to make their life a bit easier and more fun. Would you be willing to connect me to people in your network to see if I could be of help to them?"

If she says Yes, then go through the request for referrals language I outlined in Chapter 5. If she says No—and I've had only five people in all these years say No to connecting me to others—she's clearly not the type of person who is a go-giver who enjoys connecting people to things that could be of value to them. More proof that she wouldn't do well in our business! Then, of course, transition to a discussion of your products or services.

You've done a three-way call, but she won't make a decision.

Let's say you've done a three-way call with your prospect, talking through all the objections she's thrown at you and your upline, but she still won't commit to enrollment. Again, questions are your best friend.

"Mary, I know we got your questions answered on the call we did with my business partner, but I still sense that there's something keeping you from jumping in. Let's talk about that."

Get her to tell you what's going through her head. You may need to talk about the objections some more, and she may have thought of new ones. Yet beneath all the objections and all the hesitating, here's what I've found is usually at the root of it all. Either deep down she doesn't want to spend consistent time every week of her life for the next couple of years on a business of her own, or she doesn't believe enough in herself to think she can actually do it. So how do you draw this out of her with questions?

"Mary, we've talked about what suggests someone will be successful at this, so let's go through that list again.

* This is a people-centric business and clearly you love people and talking to them, so you've got that covered.

* This business requires at least ten hours a week of consistent activity. Do you still think you want to devote ten hours a week to this?

* As we've talked about, this business is simple, but you have to be coachable and willing to learn the simple system. Are you coachable?"

If Mary says Yes to all of that, then you segue into the enrollment. "Terrific, well then let's get you started."

If, however, she's still dragging her feet, you ask another question, (which can be the mother of all questions) to get at the real root of her stalling. "So if you know that you're willing to learn how to build this, Mary, and I can teach you how to build this, and there are loads of people just like you who are successfully building businesses, I must ask you, do you believe you have what it takes to do this?"

This question is so valuable because it will help you get to the root of the hesitation—you'll likely discover she lacks belief in herself. Once you know what you're dealing with, you can talk her through it.

> Ask the mother of all questions, "Do you believe you have what it takes to do this?"

"Mary, what do you think the people who are successful have that you don't have?" You may find that she simply doesn't believe enough in herself to even want to try or that she doesn't think she deserves to be successful. Yes, we hear some pretty heavy stuff. But remember, we're not therapists, and we can't make someone believe in herself. What we can assure her of is this, "I'd be honored and thrilled if I were somehow part of you learning how capable you are and that you, too, can have something successful, lucrative, and fun of your very own. Would that make you happy?"

If ultimately her answer is No to that, then let her go with love. Because you can't fix what's broken. But don't let her go without adding, "Here's what I do know would make you happy: having the best skin of your life (or better health or whatever you have to offer on the product or services side)," again sharing what's in it for her to be your customer.

Here's a real life example from my prospecting. A woman I was talking to (let's call her Sue) was dragging her feet for three weeks. I practice what I preach, so I took her through the list of what suggests success, and she answered affirmatively to all. "Well this sounds like a no-brainer fit to me, Sue," I said. "So why on Earth aren't you moving forward?"

My blunt, conversational question got her to finally share her real hesitation. Sue wasn't sure she wanted to work with that many people all the time and had a real question as to whether she wanted to "be responsible for the success of others." That was a huge red flag. Our business is all about helping others succeed, and we're looking for people who see it as a privilege and not a burden. So I was able to identify that she wasn't a good fit and I did The Take Away, but still got her as a customer on our products and got two referrals, whom she described as friends who love helping other people.

It all sounds great, but she just can't decide.

Sometimes, no matter how much you follow the conversation system, or how elegantly you carry out the questions and back-and-forth discussion, your prospect simply won't make a damn decision. They're Just. Not. Sure.

Clearly, these folks are not gunslingers; they're the anti-gunslingers. I've found the best way to get them to decide is to spoon-feed them a decision-making process. I do this by assigning simple homework.

I ask them to do a few things that they would be coached to do when they start their business anyway, telling them that the exercises will show them whether or not they really want to build their own business and, if they do, they'll actually be a little ahead of the game.

> I've found the best way to get them to decide is to spoonfeed them a decision-making process.

I tell them to do these three things:

1. "Write down your reason WHY for wanting to do this business. We've already talked about it, I know, but solidify it for yourself in writing."

2. "Sit down with a pad and pen and write down everyone you know. Then put stars by your top 30 Dream Teamers; the people you'd love to build something with, even though you have no idea if they'd be interested."

3. "I want to you to think about your WHY, and if you don't pursue this business, how else will you get to where you want to be. What's your Plan B? Write it down."

Then I set another time to talk (remember appointment to appointment!) and tell them to send their homework to me before our call—their WHY, the number of people on their list, and their Plan B to get them to their WHY. This puts them in action. It also shows if they're willing to do some work and hold up their end of the accountability bargain. Plus, if they ultimately decide this isn't for them, they've already got their list of referrals ready for you. Bam!

They've gone MIA.

It's happened to us all, probably more times than we can count. Someone expresses interest, confirms receipt of your email with more info, and perhaps even confirms the upcoming three-way call. Then you get voicemail. Your prospect has officially gone into the Witness Protection Program.

Your first thought should always be to give the person the benefit of the doubt. Things come up, accidents happen, humans forget. So you should leave a voicemail that says something like, "Hi, Mary, this is Romi. We had a call scheduled at this time to help you further explore a business with us. I want to offer you a few times when we could reschedule. I have three this afternoon or 9:30 am tomorrow; which one works for you? Text or call me back with your choice and to let me know that you're okay. Talk soon!"

If they don't get back to you, I like to follow up in a couple days via text or email with, "Hi, Mary, I'm wondering if you're still interested in continuing our conversation. If you're having a hard time telling me No, please don't give it a second thought. I don't have any attachment to your decision. I've got time to briefly talk today at X or X. Let me know which one works for you."

Still crickets? Give it a couple weeks and then, "Hi, Mary. Hope you're well. I've got to tell you, I'm really good at what I do. And I'm really good at follow up. You've told me in the past that you thought my business might be a great way for you to do (their potential WHY). So until you tell me No, I'm going to keep checking in with you every so often."

This approach takes the pressure off of them; all they have to do is tell you No if they don't want to hear any more. I've been pleasantly surprised how many times this has led to a continued conversation. "I don't want you to stop coming back to me. It's just not the right time," or "This is what I'm worried about..."

I know it's easy to let your emotions fall when people go MIA. But I want you to ask yourself this very important question: Do you really want someone on your team who doesn't show up, or has the class to give you a head's up of a conflict or a change of heart out of respect for your time? If you were hiring people for your team, and had to pay them out of your own pocket, would you extend an offer to a candidate who doesn't show up for an interview? I sure as hell wouldn't.

If you're anything like me, you've asked yourself and the universe why everyone doesn't see what we see, and why everyone doesn't return calls or show up for scheduled appointments.

But my husband and wise biz partner John often reminds me what happiness researcher and best-selling author Shawn Achor says that I hope you'll take to heart. Common knowledge doesn't mean common action. Just because they have the same info as you, it doesn't mean they're going to act on it like you. Just because you were raised or trained with social graces or business etiquette, doesn't mean they were. Don't take it personally. Don't let it drain you.

Remember that on some level, at least right now, they don't care. They're not that into you. Into this business model. Into your company. Into building something of their very own. Into doing what they know will be consistent work. And that's ok.

I'm living proof—and so is my team—that there are plenty of people out there who will be into you, and if you talk to enough people you will find them. Just promise me that you'll make all this easier on yourself and them by asking them the questions to get them to tell you their truth. Don't be afraid of No, because the No's will get you closer to the Yes's, and closer to finding the people who are way into you, our business model, your company, and building something of their very own.

Just keep talking to people. Love the process. When you talk to enough people, you will find the ones who are into you, just like I did. That's when it gets really fun. And then your people will find people who are very into them.

> I'm living proof—and so is my team—that there are plenty of people out there who will be into you, and if you talk to enough people you will find them.

I must give a shout out to everyone on our team who has said Yes. We are very into you. In fact, you're why we talk to people all the time—to find more people just like you.

CHAPTER 9

The Fortune's in the Follow-Up

One of the biggest mistakes people in our profession make is they think 'one and done.' If they talk once to someone and get a "No," they don't revisit the subject with that person again. Hopefully we all experience—and often—the bliss that comes when someone enters your funnel for the first time, and through a series of conversations over a short period of time, they purchase your products or join your team. But the majority of people you talk to will need to see and hear your message many times.

The Rule of Seven is an old marketing maxim. It advises that a person needs to see or hear your message at least seven times before she takes action. There's no proof that the number seven is universally the holy grail of touches. But what is undeniable is that marketing—and in our case, social marketing—must be an on-going process in order to be successful.

Why do people need to hear from us so many times before taking action? First, the amount of noise each of us is bombarded with every day is staggering. And on any given day, the person you're talking to may have so much noise in her life that she's not able to really listen, even if she wants to. Second, what you're talking about may be so far from what she's ever considered that it's going to take a series of exposures for her to warm up to the idea. Maybe it's not the right time because she's so busy and overwhelmed that she can't even focus on what you're telling her. And perhaps she's just not looking for what you have to offer. At least not right now.

So don't get down because the people you're talking to aren't jumping right in to become your team member or your customer. I mean really, why should you be able to defy the numbers game dictated by human behavior and our noisy world? Unless you've got superhero powers of mind manipulation, this is how it's supposed to be.

What you must remember, however, is that "No" really means "Not Right Now." There are a whole lot of statistics on the internet about how many touches it takes and how few people actually make all those touches. I've even cited them in trainings for my team. Unfortunately, in doing research for this book I learned that not only are the stats bogus, but the sales organization credited with coming up with them is bogus, too.

> Failure comes not from getting No, but from failing to keep following up with the No.

But I don't need verified research to tell you if you keep following up with people, a whole bunch of them will either buy your products or join your team. Because I've lived it. And I've heard hundreds of beautiful stories of No finally turning into Yes. Failure comes not from getting No, but from failing to keep following up with the No.

If you take away nothing else from this chapter, remember this Golden Rule: Reach back periodically to everyone you've talked to, unless they've already joined your business or told you "Don't contact me again." If you don't, you're missing a whole lot of Yes's that will happen if you just keep talking. Take note that I'm not excluding people who have said Yes to being your customer. Reaching back to your customers to talk about the business and to get referrals is vitally important. Those customers who already love your products are your lowest hanging fruit for business builders and referrals.

So why don't you consistently reach back? Most often it's because you either don't want to seem pushy, or you're so wounded after the first No that you're afraid to go back.

Repeat after me, "I'm not being pushy, I'm being professional!" Since we know people you talk to are programmed by human nature and their environment to say No the first time, their No says nothing about you.

Here's a real-life success story to inspire you. Jen Griswold ignored the messages from her childhood bestie Jamie Petersen for about six months. She wasn't interested in hearing about Jamie's new business. But Jamie was persistent and kept dripping on Jen, despite the crickets. Jen finally did a call with Jamie so she could tell her No. The call led to Jen agreeing to provide referrals to Jamie, but Jen couldn't get the business out of her head. That led to a three-way call with me, which ignited Jen's idea that she could build a team that could provide military spouses a way to build lucrative, flexible, portable businesses. Jen is an Air Force Reservist who took a long time to get to her reason WHY for wanting to do this and her Yes. Had Jamie given up, our team would've missed out on the exceptional leadership duo that is Jamie and Jen, two of the most successful leaders in our entire company.

Our last four new personal business partners and three customers are people I've been talking to for years. As in two, three, four, and five years! Over the years, they've told us No, not right now, not a good time, and even said nothing at all (those damn crickets). Had we given up, we would've missed out on all of these new additions to our business. That would've been a shame for all of us.

Reach back you must, and reach back you will.

Remember the ideas I gave you to keep your list organized? It's very important to find a system that works for you so you can keep track for reach-back purposes. If you need to, turn back now and review Chapter 3, and then decide on a system to adopt—whether it's an Excel spreadsheet, a notebook, index cards, an online system, or a massive Word doc with a table like I've used for years. I encourage you to use your calendaring system to keep you on task. I'm an iCal user (maybe you use Outlook or an old-school paper calendar). It doesn't matter what you use, just make sure you're populating upcoming follow-up appointments whenever possible.

For example, if I talk to someone today who says it's just not the right time for her because of her house remodel, I'm going to ask her when she expects the project to be finished. Then I'll tell her, "I'm going to loop back with you in five weeks. I'll look forward to hearing how great the remodel turned out, and to pick up our conversation. Sound good?" Then I'll calendar it with details, including a reminder to ask her how the remodel turned out. No matter how crazy my life is and all the things I forget, I'm not going to forget to do this.

> I like to think of reaching back to people as a game. It's fun to figure out excuses to loop back.

I like to think of reaching back to people as a game. It's fun to figure out excuses to loop back and get my prospects to think, "Ok, I should really listen to what Romi has to say." There are many reasons you can come up with to reach back, but here are seven that you should definitely be using.

Reach-Back Reason #1: To update them on your business.

Whenever you hit a big milestone, it's a great reason to loop back. Even if you perceive it as a little milestone, as long as it's forward motion, it can be talked about like a big milestone. When you earn your investment back in your first check, reach out to the people you've spoken to thus far. "I know we talked when I first launched my business and it wasn't the right time for you. But I had to tell you what's happened in just a month. I've already earned back my investment, so everything from here on will help me save for the kids' college funds/go into our vacation fund/toward a down payment on a house. I think you should take another look. This could be the way for you to (include what's in it for them based on your prior conversation)."

Maybe it's when you promote in title or earn company incentives. "I wanted to update you on my business, because I'm really seeing some traction here. Since we last talked, I've been promoted three times, which means my earnings have continued to grow, and I've earned a free trip to the Wine Country for some decadent R&R. Maybe you should take another look. It sure would be fun to help you earn extra money and perks like this."

When people on your team experience successes, it provides another compelling reason. "I had to reach out because I'm not only having great success, but I'm helping other people reach big milestones in their businesses. My business partner just received a promotion and a bonus, and she's building her business around her two kids and demanding nursing career. She's on track to be able to cut back her shifts soon. I think you should take another look at this because you could enjoy this kind of success too."

When our first attempts at talking about our new business are pretty bad to downright awful, who can blame us for not wanting to go back to the same person and try again? But we must. The numbers tell us so. And an update on your business is the perfect reason to do this.

I reached back to a number of people with whom I wasn't, shall we say, eloquent at the beginning. My approach when I reached back was one of complete honesty. "Remember how we talked about my new business a month ago? I want to be honest with you. It was all new to me and I don't think I did a very good job talking about my new gig. I probably confused the hell out of you. But now that I've got the hang of it and I'm seeing this sucker grow, I'd love a do-over so you can really understand what we're doing and how we do it. It still may not be the right fit for you, but at least we'll know. This time it won't be because I didn't explain it well, but because you don't want to grow your own side biz to bring in extra income."

Every single person I reached back to with this approach welcomed the do-over. Because I was more confident and had a more powerful posture, I had universally good conversations that led to customers, referrals, and a few new team members. And we had some great giggles about how much I sucked.

Reach-Back Reason #2: New product launches.

Well this is a no-brainer. New product launches provide the perfect opportunity to reach out to everyone you've ever talked to who never said Yes to the business. And when I say everyone, I mean it. I'm talking about people stuck in your funnel, referral sources, your customers, people who have said No (and since you're so coachable you interpreted it as "not right now"), and people who didn't say anything.

Maybe they previously mentioned they would be interested in something similar to what you're launching. "The last time we talked you said down the road you might be interested in an alternative to getting filler injections (or a weight loss aid that's gluten-free). I couldn't wait to tell you—I've got the product for you!"

If they haven't explicitly told you they'd be interested in a certain product, you know they should be based on what you know about them. When you reach back you can lead with WIIFT. "The last couple of times I've seen you at the gym, you complained of being so tired. So I had to reach out because we just launched a new formula that's been clinically proven to increase energy. I think you might want to take a look."

New product launches also provide an excellent opportunity to reignite business conversations. Because every new product offers the possibility to capture more market share. "I know you said my business wasn't the right fit for you, but I had to reach back because we just launched a new product that will help us capture more of the multi-billion-dollar anti-aging market (or whatever market your company focuses on). Since we last spoke, have you found another way to pay for your son's private school tuition? Well, maybe you should take another look at what I do. I bet you know a lot of people who would want our new product, so why shouldn't they get it from you?" This same approach works for your existing customers. Since you'll want to talk with them about your product anyway, you should also be describing the business advantage the new product brings.

Reach-Back Reason #3: An event in their city.

Of course you'll want to take advantage of events in your contacts' areas to reignite a conversation. In fact, I coach our team to use the list of our company's events that our corporate team publishes in the weekly e-newsletter as a memory jogger and a reach-back reminder.

A local event provides an organic reason to reach out and touch someone again. "I know the last time we talked, my business wasn't a good fit for you. But I had to reach out and see if you'd like to restart a conversation. There's an informal event happening in your area next week, and if you decide you want to take a closer look, it will be a great opportunity." If the answer is still "No," an upcoming local event gives you the perfect opening to ask for referrals. "I totally get it's not for you, but since we're expanding in your market, your local network is going to hear about us. If they're not going to hear about it from you, I'd love for them to hear about us and our products from me. Do you have a few more minutes to talk about exactly who I'm looking for and who in your network should hear about us?"

Reach-Back Reason #4: Good news or media coverage about your company.

When your company receives awards or media coverage, either for your products and services or your business, it's a great reason to loop back with people you've talked to before. "Hey, Maura, it's Romi. I know we've talked about my business before and it wasn't a good fit, but I thought you might want to take another look. Our CEO was just featured in Smart Business magazine talking about how our business is allowing anyone to create their own microenterprise. This is another example of mainstream business media talking about the new way of selling products, and how people like you and me get to benefit. This still might not be for you. But even if it's not, I'd love to be connected with people in your network who might be looking to start a smart business of their own in part-time hours. It's a great time for you to take a closer look and hear what I've been able to do since we last talked, don't you think?"

Reach-Back Reason #5: To be a go-giver.

One of the most helpful books on effective networking that I've ever read is *The Go-Giver* by Bob Burg and John David Mann.

Go-Givers don't just cultivate one-sided relationships, looking at people as those you can get something from. Instead, Go-Givers give to people by being helpful, being a connector, being genuinely interested in others, and singing other's praises. It's all about how you can serve. It's the simple, golden principle of life that I teach our team and our kids—whatever you put out in the world is what you get back. Give to others and they'll give to you.

In order to be a Go-Giver to people in your network, you have to learn about them and keep good

> It's all about how you can serve.

notes about what you learn. That's why, in addition to finding out someone's pain points are and how your business can eliminate their pain, you want to ask questions and listen. So you can discover and remember what's of interest to them and send them things that they'd like to receive.

When I collect contact info (aka "digits") from somebody, maybe on an airplane or at the side of a swimming pool, after we part ways I write down notes about them, either on their business card, in the notes field of their contact entry, or in a little notebook I carry with me at all times. Later I enter the info into a spreadsheet I have with all of my contacts, with one column dedicated to details about them.

I capture things like if they've told me they're looking for a really good babysitter. Or maybe they are going to be moving to another city and I happen to know people, and I want to hook them up. Maybe I just wrote down what they do for a living, and then any time I come across something that could be of interest or use to them, I loop back with them and offer it to them.

Here are some real life examples from my business. I talked to a nurse from Northern California who I met while skiing at

Lake Tahoe. She wasn't interested in our business because she was so busy, she felt like she didn't even have time for a shower every day. We laughed and promised to keep in touch.

Three months later I read a really interesting article about nursing and healthcare, and it quoted healthcare experts and practitioners from her area. I forwarded her that article and I said, "This article made me think of you, and I thought you'd find it interesting. You might even know some of the folks quoted. I'm enjoying keeping up with you on Facebook; it looks like your son's birthday party was a blast! Happy Spring!"

That led to, "Wow, thanks so much for thinking of me, Romi." Then we started chitchatting a little bit about birthday parties, and then the conversation turned to if she was still busy. She admitted that my business was very attractive to her, but she just couldn't imagine being able to devote time to a side gig. It did lead, however, to me being able to ask her for referrals, which she happily forked over, and a discussion of how her sensitive skin had flared up because of stress. I was, of course, happy to get her on our products and still have a devoted customer and walking billboard.

Here's another example. I had been trying to get referrals out of a small business owner for a long time, but she wasn't connecting me to anyone in her network. She knows tons of people throughout the U.S., and people respect her. I genuinely love her business, so it was authentic for me to start giving her social media shout-outs, and connecting her to potential customers and strategic business partners. I even helped her find her seasonal temp employee.

She thought that I was genuinely interested in her succeeding, and she was right. It makes me so happy to help other entrepreneurs and other women. She started throwing business my way, even without me asking. I gained a few customers and a business partner. And we both have the warm glow that comes from knowing we helped, and continue to help, a fellow entrepreneur grow.

Reach-Back Reason #6: Pregnant, new baby or kids starting school.

One of the reasons many women want to build their own turn-key businesses is to eventually create the freedom to be with their kids more. So I've found that even when people have said No, they sometimes see WIIFT a little differently once they have a bun in the oven or a new baby they have to leave at home to go to work.

When a friend who works announces she's pregnant, in addition to being genuinely excited and interested and providing some fun and helpful articles or resources, I always ask how long she plans to

> They sometimes see WIIFT a little differently once they have a bun in the oven or a new baby.

take off after the baby. This inevitably leads to a conversation where either a) she laments that she doesn't get enough time off, or b) she's excited that she'll have three months off and doesn't want to even think about how she'll manage when she goes back. This conversation gives me the opening to suggest she might want to take another look at what I do. "You know, between now and when the baby comes, you could build a significant start to a lucrative business that could give you more options down the road. A professional life that fits in around your baby, not the other way around."

In what I like to call "Post-Partum Prospecting," whenever one of my friends who work gives birth, I mark on my calendar to reach out to her four months after she delivers. I know how hard it is to leave your baby at home and go back to work after your maternity leave. It's gut wrenching. I remember the first day I had to go back to work after Nate was born and I cried all the way to work, and then at lunch, and then when I had him back in my arms.

So of course I'm keeping in contact with my friend before her maternity leave is over, to be a Go-Giver with tips, support for sleeplessness, and genuine appreciation for the never-ending stream of pictures chronicling a new baby's every move. But I've found that after they've been back at work for a month, they likely would love to talk about how they could be home all the time, and they're back in the swing of things enough to be able to entertain adding something else to their plates. This approach has led to loads of new mamas or soon-to-be mamas on our team.

Reach-Back Reason #7: When someone just like them succeeds.

I think this is the easiest one to do. You want to go back to people in your funnel when someone just like them does something noteworthy. When somebody just like them joins your team. "Hey, Lisa. It's Romi, and I was just thinking of you, because I had a teacher join my team last night. My new business partner Mary is really excited for me to help her build a business that will match or exceed her teaching salary so she can ultimately spend more time with her kids. I couldn't help but wonder if you wanted to take another look at our business, since I know you would love to drop all the tutoring you do over the summer."

> Go back to people in your funnel when someone just like them does something noteworthy.

Also reach back when somebody just like them promotes or earns incentives. You better believe that every time a real estate pro earns a free Lexus or a luxury trip in our company, I reach out to every person I know in real estate. The same for every other demographic. "A Realtor that I work with is celebrating huge success in our business, so I thought of you. She just earned a free Lexus and a trip to Maui, and she's giddy over the perks that she doesn't get in her day job. I thought you might want to take another look at what we do. If the perks don't excite you, maybe adding an income stream that's insulated from the ups and downs in the market will."

Another compelling reason is when somebody just like them retires from their day job because of their side gig income. "Tammy, I had to reach out to you because there's an accountant I work with who retired from her firm because her side business has grown so big. She's so excited not to have to go through another tax season. I thought maybe you'd want to take another look at what we're doing."

Now let's get you reaching back.

Get in Action

Every day for the next six days, pick one of the reasons we've covered and think about who you can reach back to using that reason as a hook. Shoot for at least three people for each reason. Incorporate this exercise into your weekly activities, even making one day each week "Reach-Back Day." You'll train yourself to constantly think of reasons, and make it a routine part of your business.

Just follow-up. If you don't, you're leaving money on the table and you're preventing yourself from building a business that could set you free. So to light a fire under your follow-up butts, I leave you with this thought. How pissed are you going to be if you reached out four times to someone, but it was another business builder who reached out on the fifth exposure (when it was the right time for your prospect), and she joins **that** person's team or becomes **her** customer? She should've been yours. Make sure she always is.

CHAPTER 10

The Key to Duplication

Growing a successful team and a lucrative income requires duplication. This means adding customers and business partners, who in turn add customers and business partners. The million-dollar question then, and the one I hear all the time, is how do we duplicate?

It's simpler than you think. And the more complicated you make it, the slower you will grow. So let's talk about how to keep it simple and multiply, as I've affectionately referred to our team, like bunnies in love.

It starts with you.

The only part of this business that we have total control over is our own activity. Now, if you're a control freak like me (I come by it honestly; you should meet my mother), this lack of control thing going on in our business can be very frustrating. So if you happen to be a bit of a control freak, I encourage you to get over it like I had to, and do it now. Because duplication, and ultimately success, in this business starts with us.

I want you to ask yourself a very simple but important question: If everyone on your team did exactly what you currently do every day, every week, and every month, how big would your business be?

Whenever you find yourself frustrated because your business isn't growing, ask yourself that question.

I still ask myself that very question. Whenever I'm noticing our team growth isn't as rapid or as steep as I would like to see, I first look at what I'm personally doing.

Here's the short list of what you should be doing to start the duplication process:

* Constantly adding to your list
* Reaching out and reaching back to people on your list
* Inviting people interested in the business to three-way calls or events and, if it's the right fit, adding them to your team
* Adding those not interested in the business as customers and asking them for referrals
* Getting paid

If you do all these things all the time, you'll teach your team how to do the same by simply duplicating your behavior. There's one more that's really important:

* Having fun

I've learned that people ultimately will join your team because of you and your energy. One of the things that attract people to us is not just the potential financial gain, but also the emotional gain. Yes, the satisfaction of building something of their own, but also having something in their life that is different, a new adventure that can be a fun outlet for them. So make sure you're having fun, because if you're not, they're going to know it.

Here's an interesting thing about personal activity that my beloved business partner Bridget Cavanaugh figured out crunching the data on her team. Your people will do, on average, half of what you do. And those are the "runners." I looked at our team over the years and damn, she's right on. I call this the Half Rule. Now of course there are exceptions to this rule, outliers who may do as much or more than a big-producing leader. I hope that you find a few of them. But they're rare. Not unicorn rare, but pretty darn close. So assume the Half Rule applies to you.

Let's assume then that you're doing the bare minimum to earn a check. The Half Rule says your peeps will do half of that. Which is pretty pathetic.

That's why to build big you must commit today to be the top producer on your team. Then commit to besting yourself every month. To show your team how it's done.

That's what I did. Early on, I recognized that I couldn't ask my team to do anything I wasn't willing to do. I consistently talked to people, and each and every month added customers and business partners. My personal volume kept going up and up. I had to set the pace and then see who kept up. Those were the ones who would get my time.

> **To build big you must commit today to be the top producer on your team.**

Team members come to me all the time with some variation of this frustration: "I'm doing all the stuff you coach us to do, but nothing is happening. My team isn't duplicating. They're not reaching out to people; they're not bringing me three-way calls."

Here's what I tell them. If someone isn't reaching out and talking, you want to try and find out why, and really have their best interests at heart. A conversation that goes something like, "Lisa, I remember you told me you desperately want to get out of teaching because you're so tired of the pink slips and you'd rather spend more time with your kids than with everybody else's children. As we discussed, this is a great vehicle for you to do that. But it's not going to fall from the sky, honey. It's going to require you to get out of your comfort zone and actually make those calls. So let's talk about why you're not doing it. Is it because you're having a hard time fitting it into your schedule? Is it because you're really still unsure of what to say? Is it because you're not sure you're in the right business? Let's get real here. You can be totally honest with me. That's how I can help you."

You'll add team members, or maybe already have, who ultimately don't want to do the consistent heavy lifting required to build this. That's okay. Because if you've done what you're supposed to do as their upline business partner to get them started strong, and you've taught them how to do all the things you're supposed to be doing, then you've done your job. Have a real conversation with them about what they really want to do with this, and let them know that they're still not matching (or half-matching your effort), then the rest is up to them.

We can teach. We can coach. We can inspire. We can collaborate. We can laugh. We can have fun together. We can dream. We can plan. But we can't motivate. That has to come from within each of us.

Of course, we owe it to our new business partners to work closely with them to teach them the basic skills and system so they can duplicate. As long as they show up and match our efforts, we will help them have a strong start. After learning the basics, the best way to teach our people how to grow is by doing three-way calls with them and their prospects, and helping to strategize with them as they start building a team. But this requires that they actually commit to consistent IPA—talking to people to find those interested enough to want to learn more. If a team member isn't doing that, there's nothing we can do for them.

Want a big, successful, and exponentially-growing business? Then keep adding to your list, reaching out to people, using three-way calls and events and pulling them through your funnel to make a decision, enrolling business partners, adding customers, and getting paid. Keep doing that and you will grow and grow, and you'll share your success and experiences with your team, which shows them how to do the same thing. If you have fun, keep doing all of that over and over—wash, rinse, repeat—then you'll find the people who are self-motivated, who see what you see and are willing to get out of their comfort zone, and do the heavy lifting to do all those things. Then they will find people who are motivated and want to build as well. That's how you duplicate.

There may be a few of you out there who are thinking right now, "That's it? Really?" Yep, that's it. So go forth and multiply like bunnies in love. It all starts with you.

CHAPTER 11

The Bullshit
We Tell Ourselves

By now I hope you have a good idea how to handle prospects' objections. But there are other objections that can be harder to overcome. Because these are the ones that you throw at yourself, and they're keeping you from building a huge business that can set you free.

There are a million different reasons you can come up with why this won't work for you. Or why you won't grow it really big. I want to explore the most common excuses you and your team members may be telling yourselves about why you're not building the businesses you say you want to. I'm going to call bullshit on each and every one. I'll also show you what's really behind these excuses, and how you can move past them and onto the real exciting work of this life—becoming the person you were meant to be.

I don't have time for this.

Let's tackle the most prevalent bullshit in our profession first. You may be saying, "I'm unable to consistently do this because I don't have time." But let's be honest. What you're really saying is, "I haven't made this a priority." Until this business is a priority, you will have time management problems, and it will be easy to avoid working your business.

We find time for everything that's important to us. Think about it. The vacation that you just didn't think you could fit in because of the mountain of work you had to do. Going to your child's soccer game even though it meant moving four other meetings. Staying up to watch *Game of Thrones* even though it meant you wouldn't get your seven hours of sleep. A blowout appointment scrunched into an already packed day so you'll look fab at the dinner party. Whatever inconvenience or painful consequences that came from making these things happen were outweighed by your desire to do them.

The next time you find yourself saying "I don't have time," instead try saying "It's not a priority," and see how that feels. "I don't have time to make calls to three new people today" becomes "It's not a priority for me to make calls to three new people today." If it's not a priority, that's totally cool. This is your business and your life. But don't kid yourself or your business partners that you want to build a huge business when you're not really willing to make it a top priority.

> The next time you find yourself saying "I don't have time," instead try saying "It's not a priority," and see how that feels.

Remember we thoroughly explored in Chapter 2 that clearly your WHY has to be big enough to outweigh any pain or inconvenience that comes from building this sucker. Maybe your WHY *is* big enough, and you *are* making time for your business, but you find that your business just isn't growing. It could be because you're spending your time in the *wrong place*.

The number one thing you have to make time for is personal prospecting. We've already talked about the essential truth that the vast majority of your time should go toward your personal recruiting and training your newbies—at least 80%. You've also learned that you also must pay yourself first by doing your prospecting and recruiting work first, so no matter what else happens to your schedule, you've taken care of what you can personally control. This ensures that you have an endless stream of people looking at your business, joining your business, and growing a business of their own.

But you may argue that with all the other team responsibilities, you just can't get to it. Let me be clear: the number one responsibility you have for your team is to set a pace and a duplication model that your team can follow.

Intellectually, I think all of this makes sense to you and thousands upon thousands of people just like you. So why don't you have enough time to reach out and talk to people?

Because it's hard. And as humans we'll do anything and everything to avoid the hard stuff. But here's the thing: it's the hard stuff that's the most important. Trust me, I'm not immune to this. In fact, it happens to me all the time. Like while I'm writing this chapter.

In the last hour, instead of focusing solely on getting my thoughts about bullshit from my head through my fingers and onto the page, I have:

> So why don't you have enough time to reach out and talk to people? Because it's hard. But here's the thing: it's the hard stuff that's the most important.

1) Checked Facebook direct messages and sent two
2) Checked email and responded to three
3) Sent a reminder email to my guest on this week's team training call
4) Made a blowout appointment (which I remembered to do after typing "blowout appointment")
5) Got up to order an iced tea (a girl can't write when she's thirsty)
6) Updated our grocery list
7) Checked to see who had RSVP'd for our summer party
8) Went to the bathroom (too much iced tea)

Why did I do all this when I had specifically carved out two hours of power writing time for myself? Why, even when I was sequestered at a Starbucks with no kids, dog, house stuff, or anyone I knew to distract me, did I not take those two hours and get this chapter written? Because writing is hard.

But wait, I went to journalism school, I was a lawyer, I was a PR exec. Writing is what I've done for a living. "But this is different," the little voice in my head says. "This is YOU putting yourself out there. And it might suck and no one will get help from it, and they'll figure out you don't know what the hell you're talking about." In other words, writing this book makes me vulnerable. My tender underbelly is exposed for the whole world to poke at.

To be perfectly honest, this whole book would've been done and to the publisher months ago if it weren't so damn hard to put myself out there and so damn easy to avoid the hard stuff.

But enough about me, let's get back to you. I'll bet you $1,000 that you're doing everything else in your business *before* you're talking to people about your business. All the other stuff you think is so necessary for the growth of your empire that is taking your available time away from talking to people. Because when you talk to people about your business and your hopes and dreams, you're putting yourself out there. Open. Vulnerable. You're opening yourself up to rejection. In other words, it's **hard**.

It's so much easier to reach out and have a "coaching call" with one of your team members to tell them the very same things you've already told them and that they've already heard on several training calls. It's much easier to call up your accountability partner and complain about the latest out-of-stock product. Or once again tell the team member to reach out and talk to three new people a day, because she still isn't doing it. Well guess what, sister, neither are you!

Let's get really clear on what you're supposed to do to grow a lucrative business:

* Reach out and talk to people about your business and your products, and find those who are looking for what you have to offer. This is where the vast majority of your time is spent—at least 80%.
* Train your newbies on the basics.
* Do three-way calls for your newbies and your other direct business partners.
* Strategize with your runners about how to support those on their team who are jogging and running.
* Recognize and praise accomplishment.

Get in Action

Over the next week, I challenge you to make a list of all the things you spend time doing for your business and the actual time you spend doing it. I think you'll be amazed where your time is going, and where it's not going. Then take a red pen to all the things that don't fall into one of the above categories. Finally, schedule in the hard stuff—dedicated time to reach out and talk to people about your business and your products.

I'm talking to enough people.

Let's say you're finding the time to talk to people. Fantastic! That's a start. But another big ole piece of BS we tell ourselves is that we're talking to *enough* people.

I was co-hosting a training series for some up-and-comers on our team, and my direct business partner Dorrit Karl, who's now one of the top leaders on our team, was participating. The class was challenged to double the amount of people they reached out to in one week. Dorrit took the challenge and could not believe the flutter of activity that it generated in her business in just seven days.

She was scheduling three-way calls because of her new reach-outs, and scheduling more follow-ups by reaching back to more people who had previously said "No" or "not right now." She added more business partners and customers in that week than she had in the prior five weeks combined! After she reported her progress on the weekly class conference call, she was asked what the difference was this week. Dorrit then said something that has become legendary in our company: "I didn't know I wasn't talking to enough people until I started talking to enough people." Preach.

Like many of you, Dorrit had tricked herself into thinking that she was really talking to enough people. In reality, she only had a few people in her funnel. But she had fooled herself into thinking she was really busy. "The exercise was a slap in the face," she admitted. "It changed the way I work my business for good."

Dorrit started to follow a daily reach-out system that many of us follow, which was formalized by another one of our team members at the tippy top of our company, Marissa McDonough. (She's a fellow Butte, Montana native and one of the coolest women I know, so I have a real soft spot for her.) It's called the "5-3-2 Method." Like everything else in this business that works, it's simple. Reach out to five new people a day, follow-up with three people in your funnel, and quickly check in with two of your business partners, even if it's just a quick text of encouragement or a shout out on Facebook.

This activity not only led Dorrit to reengage in her business, it also caused her excitement and her belief to grow. She became more confident, which made her more effective in prospecting and more magnetic. It's no surprise that she started seeing consistent results. She talked her way into a free Lexus, luxurious trips for her and her husband Scott to Hawaii and London and to the top of our company. Her team's duplication and her paycheck continue to increase.

So if you or a team member isn't growing, or even worse, is going backwards, ask yourself (or your team member):

* How many times have you presented the opportunity this week?
* How many three-way calls have you done this week?

You can't BS those numbers. Here's what I know after growing a seven-figure business: if you're not adding business partners and customers, you're most likely not talking to enough people. So make sure you're actually talking to new people. Every. Damn. Day. That's how you find people who want to use your products and who want to learn more about your business. Which means you will be bringing your upline three-way calls. Which means you'll be adding business partners. And this is what you'll model for your entire team. This biz is a numbers game and there's no way to bullshit the numbers.

> This biz is a numbers game and there's no way to bullshit the numbers.

I've recruited enough people.

Maybe you've been telling yourself, "Hey, I've been working the numbers game. I've recruited 20 (or 30 or 40) people and I'm not where I should be (or thought I would be)." Let's think about this for a minute. If it only took recruiting that small number, wouldn't you hear about the enormous success stories in this business channel all the time? We don't, so that must not be enough.

My friend Richard Bliss Brooke, who is a living legend in our profession, has studied how many people it takes to build big. He's talked to hundreds and hundreds of successful network marketing professionals, and here's what he found we all have in common. We recruited at least 100 people in our first two years. If you're in the third year of your business and you've recruited fewer than 50 people and you aren't where you want to be, there's your big clue.

I challenge you to commit to bring on 25 people in the next six months. And then 25 more people in the next six months. That would be 50 people in a year. So what if you fall short? You'll shoot for the moon, but land among the stars. You'll still be much closer to your goal than you are now. Among those new peeps, you'll have found people who have come to play big. And your bank account will definitely be happier for all your efforts.

I'm being coachable, but nothing is happening.

I'm sure you think you're being coachable, and you may in fact really be trying to be coachable. But if you were 100% coachable, you'd be seeing success. Are you really talking to enough people, leading with the business and defaulting to the products? Are you hiding behind email and texting to talk to your network or are you picking up the damn phone like you're coached? Are you being consistent, touching your business every day? Are you having faith in the three-way call? Are you working on what's between your ears every day? The answers to these questions, when you answer them honestly, will tell you what's wrong.

Ok, maybe you have been coachable, but you've been receiving really bad coaching. That's not your fault, and I'm sorry that's happened to you. Just be really glad you found this book.

Because I've seen over and over that when people follow what I've laid out in this book, their business grows. And they have a lot of fun in the process.

> **If you were 100% coachable, you'd be seeing success.**

I've got a runner.

This is something that drives me absolutely batshit crazy; it's common BS we tell ourselves that completely screws with our heads, and ultimately our business.

I hear this all the time, "Oh my God, I've got a runner (or superstar or insert whatever noun you want to use to describe someone who is going faster than the average)." But the reality is that their "runner" has been stuck at the minimum personal volume to be commissionable for three months in a row. OK people, that's not a runner or a superstar or a rockstar. That's a dabbler who is doing the minimum required to earn commission in a pay plan. That's mediocre at best.

A runner is someone who follows the system to the letter. Who reaches out to new people all the time, who brings you multiple three-ways every week. Who adds new business partners every single month and doesn't stop. That's a runner. It's kind of like Dorrit with the talking. You won't know what a runner is until you have one. So until you find one, just trust me.

You must routinely take inventory of what you have in order to know how far you have to go to reach your goals. That requires you to be realistic about what you really have. If you're fooling yourself that you have runners, superstars, and others who are *en fuego* (a.k.a. wholesale customers, dabblers, and hobbyists), you'll slow down your activity. And this will keep you from finding the people out there who are going to run with you.

Another reason we mischaracterize or exaggerate the activity and commitment of those on our teams is because it makes it easier to justify spending your time coaching them instead of doing the hard stuff. I'm sorry, but once you stop doing all this "coaching" (a.k.a. pleading, dragging, carrying), you will have a whole bunch of time back on your plate to reach out and talk to people with skin, and find the right folks. So get real with yourself and your team. Stop dicking around. Do the hard stuff and grow your wealth.

I can only sell products.

Wrong. That's total BS. The real problem is that you're leading with the products and not talking enough about the business. Remember, the vast majority of the time, we lead with the business and default to the products. There are two reasons why people won't lead with the business. Either you feel insecure when talking about the business or you're simply not coachable. So if you're not leading with the business, ask yourself which one applies to you.

But here's the inescapable truth: you get what you ask for. If you don't talk about the business, you'll never add business partners. Plus, the conversation flow simply won't work if you lead with the product. If you talk to someone about the products and they say, No I don't want to use your products, how on Earth can you transition to, "Well how about considering building a business with these products you have no interest in?"

> You get what you ask for. If you don't talk about the business, you'll never add business partners.

There are countless stories in our company about people who added customers and never mentioned the business. Yet they're incensed when the customer tells them they want to join another builder's team. Well tough luck, chick, the other builder actually had a business conversation with them.

If you're leading with the products, you're likely doing it because it feels safe. It's comfortable. The important thing to figure out is why it's uncomfortable for you to lead with the business. *That's* what you should be working on.

I don't need three-way calls.

Oh this is some major league bullshit. You need to use them whether you're brand spanking new or a seasoned veteran of the profession. If you don't believe me, go back and reread Chapter 6.

I don't have the right network.

Again, bullshit! You're pre-judging. You really have no idea what someone wants or needs or may be looking for until you have a conversation with them. You have no idea who will actually grow this thing. People have said to me that they never thought in a million years I'd be building a network marketing business. And I could say that about some of our most valuable players on my team.

Who does have the right network? Anyone with big enough balls to reach out and have conversations with people they know and people they get referred to. More times than not, when you offer up this excuse, what you're really saying is, "I'm too chicken to reach out to the people who could really run with this and make themselves and me a fortune." You may also be saying, and this greatly saddens me, "I don't think I'm worthy of great success."

I don't want to be THAT person who people want to run from.

Phewww! I don't want you to be THAT person either. Somehow, somewhere, you got it in your head that reaching out to people about your business and your products is bothering them. But what if you knew that the next person you message on Facebook to start a conversation desperately needs to earn more money so she can get out of a broken marriage?

What if the next person you run into around town is living in a fancy house that she can no longer afford and is going to the food bank to feed her girls?

What if the next person you call is trying to recapture an identity outside of mom and wife, and misses the social, intellectual, and financial benefits of working, but needs flexibility?

These are REAL stories from our team, and they're all driving free Starfire Pearl Sexi Lexi now. (Yes, that's really how we sometimes refer to the free Lexus cars we get. We take this all *very* seriously.)

For the right people, you have a gift. Don't decide for someone else whether they need that gift. Think highly enough of them to let them decide. You already learned that just by being a human, they're programmed to say No. So if they say No, don't take it personally. Move onto the next person and remember to reach back to follow up with the No's. We have a whole bunch of Lexus earners who said No first, but really meant "not right now."

I don't want to work from appointment to appointment because I don't want to be pushy.

Working from appointment to appointment is not pushy. It's another "P" word. **Professional.** Your time is valuable and so is your prospect's time. Stop pussyfooting around and efficiently lead your prospects through the process of discovering if this is a good fit for them. If you don't set appointments, you'll be chasing people. Which will undoubtedly make you feel pushy and like one of "those people." So save yourself some grief, treat others like you'd want to be treated and be professional.

This should be easier.

Why? I think you're confusing simple with easy. Yes, our business is incredibly simplistic, but that doesn't mean it's easy. Give me an example of another incredibly rewarding endeavor that's easy. Marriage, parenthood, earning an advanced degree, running a marathon, getting and staying in good shape. Are any of these easy? No, they're hard work.

And also incredibly rewarding.

> Our business is incredibly simplistic, but that doesn't mean it's easy.

So why would you think that building your own six- or seven-figure business would be easy?

It's true that it's far easier to build this sucker than having to build an entire infrastructure and everything else that usually goes into creating a business of your own from the ground up. Certainly easier than that. But not easy.

So stop bitching it's not easier, and just work harder and smarter. I love this quote from entrepreneur, investor, film producer, author, TV star and philanthropist Mark Cuban who knows a few things about being successful. "Work like there is someone working 24 hours a day to take it away from you." In other words, consistently work your ass off and you'll see success. It ain't complicated.

I don't have what it takes to be a leader.

You may be telling yourself that "successful people" have talents, experience and access to things that you don't. The never-ending stream of success stories in our profession, of people with every type of background imaginable, proves that this is utter bullshit.

What you're really telling yourself is that you don't believe you have what it takes to lead or that you don't deserve success. If you're carrying around these harmful beliefs, you're not alone. These doubts can, and do, plague people, from women with accomplished corporate careers all the way to stay-at-home moms who've never worked outside the home. It's a lot more common than I ever imagined.

But I'm calling bullshit on this also. Award-winning college football offensive line coach Jason MacEndoo sums it up nicely, "Leadership is about influence—nothing more, nothing less. Leaders are agents of change that add value to those around them and make a positive impact in their organization. Good leaders inspire their followers to have confidence in them. But great leaders inspire their followers to have confidence in themselves." [MacEndoo, J. (2013). "Do Hard Times Create Good Leaders?" Mountains & Minds Magazine.]

Leadership isn't complicated. Anyone can be a leader in this profession by showing your team how to build. You do that by building your business. Walk the walk and talk the talk. If you're willing to do everything it takes to duplicate in this business, then you will inspire. Then, without even trying to lead, that's exactly what you'll be doing. It's about simply having confidence in ourselves, believing we're worthy, and taking action to reach our goals. That's what inspires others.

I will make mistakes.

Ok, this one isn't BS. You *will* make mistakes. You *will* fail. But the bullshit part of this is that somehow you're telling yourself that you're not supposed to make mistakes to be successful, or that somehow there are other humans who are anointed at birth with immunity from screwing up, coming up short or falling flat.

Here's the thing. None of us are immune from failure, and thank God for that. Because I've learned as an entrepreneur, a wife, a parent, a sister and a human, that we can't learn how to do anything really well without making mistakes. A major business crush of mine, Sir Richard Branson, is full of pearls of wisdom on the importance of failure. Whenever I've stepped in it, I've replayed his often quoted, Tweeted and posted wise words in my head: "Failure is simply indispensable to the entrepreneurial experience," and "Nobody gets everything right every time, and it is how we learn from our mistakes that defines us."

When I screw up—and I do just about every day in some part of my life—I do an exercise that takes just a few minutes and is a tremendous help. I encourage you to try it. Stop and think about what happened, why it happened, and what you can learn from it. Then let it go. Be kind to yourself. This exercise has proven invaluable to not only helping me avoid the same mistake again, but also to gaining insights that help me be a better, happier, and more fulfilled human.

When you and those you work with make mistakes, have grace with them and yourself. Because we're all works in progress. How exciting is that?

> When you and those you work with make mistakes, have grace with them and yourself. Because we're all works in progress.

It's saturated where I live/this biz just doesn't work in our town/I don't have anyone near me to help me.

I just howl when I hear these BS excuses. I started my business in the thriving metropolis of Bozeman, Montana, population 39,000. I was the first consultant from my company in the state, so I had no local support. But I started talking to people and added Nicole Cormany. Then we were a party of two. I added fellow Bozemanite Bridget Cavanaugh who had contacts all over the country. Before long we were a party of ten. Then 30. And it just kept growing exponentially from there. We were living in this gorgeous little hamlet, building our business not only in Bozeman and around Montana, but also around the country. Southern California started growing in a big way because of Tracy Willard, a Bozeman teacher Nicole brought on board, who was originally from Orange County. Spokane, Washington started to blow up with three future Lexus earners and their teams, because Nicole's husband Josh grew up with Amy Byrd, who lived there. Bridget's tentacles reached out to Denver, Jackson Hole, Washington, DC, and Dallas, and those teams reached out around the country.

As the team has grown through the years, we've of course added huge teams in large metropolitan areas around the country and now in Canada. But we've also seen big success stories coming from small towns. Jessica Zuroff, one of our team's top leaders, had a meteoric start to her business that kept going, and now she's at the very top of our company. She lives in Hebron, North Dakota. Population 747. Try telling Jessica that size matters!

> **One of our team's top leaders lives in Hebron, North Dakota. Population 747. Try telling Jessica that size matters!**

On the other hand, don't think that just because your market has loads of network marketing professionals, whether in your company or in other companies, that it's going to affect your business. One thing our Bozeman team taught us is that there's plenty of room to grow, since everyone has different networks and different spheres of influence. That's why at one point there were three Lexus earners living in the same neighborhood in Bozeman, with a fourth just a mile down the road. It's why there are four enormously successful team members who started out at the same elementary school in Amarillo, Texas.

I remember going to our company's first convention—just three months in and very green—and walking up to the then

VP of Sales, the late, great Chris Diaz, to introduce myself. I told him that I was going to build Montana so big one day that he'd be forced to come from warm Florida to the frozen tundra to support my team. He let out one of his deep laughs that always ended in a high-pitched giggle, and said with his Cuban accent, "These businesses don't grow big in places like Montana."

Chris knew exactly what he was doing. He immediately recognized that I was hungry, had a big fire in my belly and loved a challenge. By telling me that piece of bullshit, he knew he was going to be throwing gasoline on my fire and getting me to run even faster. I replied, "Watch me. I'll have you on a horse one day."

I never did get Chris to Montana and on that horse. He got sick with cancer and passed away far too soon, leaving behind a beautiful family and the thousands of people in our profession he touched. But I'll never forget what he whispered in my ear the night I received the two top awards at our company's second convention just a year later. "I knew you would build it. I just knew you could do it. I knew a woman like you doesn't believe in excuses."

I don't want you to believe in excuses either. We have such a short time here. At the end of our days, do we want to look back and know we were brave and audacious, or do we want to have lived a life of excuses? As Chris was best known for teaching all of us, "You're exceptional and bound for greatness." Don't let excuses get in the way of that.

All these stories you're making up in your head are a complete waste of time and energy. They're just excuses. When we make excuses like this, we're really just scared we're not good enough or worthy of great success. What are your limiting beliefs about yourself? Where do they come from? Past failures? What you were told growing up? What you were told yesterday by the prospect who said she thought your business was stupid?

> Do we want to look back and know we were brave and audacious, or do we want to have lived a life of excuses?

The truth is, we each have everything within ourselves to succeed. But in this business, you have to have a few other really important things. Hunger. The willingness to be completely coachable and learn how to do this. Consistency. The willingness to be uncomfortable. And the resilience to keep going in the face of No's and disappointments.

It's so sad how many businesses fail before they're even started, or blocked from becoming the huge success stories they can be, because of the excuses we tell ourselves. How many times have you told yourself you can't do something that countless other people can?

Every time you put out an excuse, you place another cement block in the walls you're building around yourself. With each excuse, you're trapping yourself in a prison of mediocrity of your own creation, condemning yourself to a life you really don't want. Being in that box may feel safe, but over time what's going to be in there with you is a whole lot of regret, what if's, shame and loneliness.

What I've learned working with thousands of people of all different backgrounds, skill sets and personality types is that we can conquer the negative voices and recognize the BS for what it is—just a load of crap. We can pull the cement blocks down, let the light in and increase our possibilities. We can get out of our own way and get on with the business of building our future and stepping into our greatness.

CHAPTER 12

Karma's a Bitch
if You Are

I couldn't write a book about how to build a business that will give you the life of your dreams without including a chapter on playing nicely with others. Because some people don't. Play nicely that is. They make this incredibly fun, collaborative, nirvana of a profession not as fun, and they make all of us look bad. I don't want you to be one of those people.

Please know that what we're talking about here isn't intended to chastise or scare anyone. In fact, these kinds of shenanigans, at least in my personal experience, are the exception and not the rule. Because I always like to give others the benefit of the doubt, I first assume these lapses in judgment occur because folks don't know any better. So let's talk about the basics of how we should be treating each other and our businesses to protect everyone, and then we'll all know better.

Let's start with the Golden Rule that's found in nearly every human culture and religion: Treat others as you want others to treat you. This is not only a great way to live, it should be the guiding principle for your business. If that's not enough to get you to play nicely, how about the karma principle? What we put out in the world is what we get back. Our business requires us to step into our greatness, and to help and inspire others to step into their greatness too. Since this is a business of duplication, and everything we do duplicates, wouldn't you want to duplicate kindness, generosity, professionalism, and ethical actions? Isn't that what you want to be surrounded by? I know I do.

What if you bump into others?

It's going to happen at some point. You talk to someone who's already been talking to another business builder in your company. If you discover that the person you're talking to has heard about your company before, then do the right thing and push her back. Tell them how great this gig is, how wonderful your products or services are, and that they should trip over themselves to get in touch with the other business builder. It doesn't matter if you know or don't know the other business builder, or if you like her or not. Don't analyze, rationalize, or intellectualize. Just push her back. Because that's exactly what you'd want someone to do for you.

> If you discover that the person you're talking to has heard about your company before, then do the right thing and push her back.

Even if the person she's already talked to is in your upline, I implore you not to believe the horseshit rationalization that it's ok to ignore the prior conversations because you're on her team and this benefits her as well. I'm here to tell you, sister, we do care. And we are capable of figuring out if it makes sense to put a prospect of ours as a customer or business partner under you. Plus, that's how you'd want to be treated by your team, right?

If you do push the person back, but she says she doesn't want to purchase from or work with the other person, then what you do next isn't so black or white. If the prospect doesn't have a relationship with the other business builder, but they had, for example, a Facebook messaging convo a year ago and there was no follow-up, you can feel comfortable moving forward with the discussion.

If someone you're talking to has an ongoing relationship with another business builder in your company, but the prospect is uncomfortable pursuing a professional relationship with her, then I suggest putting the responsibility on the prospect to have a conversation with the other consultant before moving forward. Require her to tell the other builder that she's decided to pursue a working relationship with someone else and offer authentic reasons. I've heard many team members worry that putting the onus on the prospect is risky, because she might not want to have what could be an uncomfortable conversation and may decide not to pursue the business. I believe, and experience has proven, that if the prospect isn't willing to have a frank, professional discussion with the other business owner, she doesn't really have the cajones to build this sucker, or the respect for you to keep you clean and start your relationship off on the right foot.

On occasion, someone you don't know and aren't even Facebook friends with may contact you out of the blue about your company. That's a fabulous, fun surprise! Always ask how they've heard about our company and our products, which helps you to discover if there have been prior conversations and people you need to push her back to. I must warn you, however, that asking the right questions doesn't always lead to the truth. So in those cases, you have to go with your gut to tell you what's right.

When you ignore your gut, that's when you get into trouble. Let me tell you about the time when I didn't listen to my gut and made a terrible decision. Learn from my awful lapse in judgment.

> **When you ignore your gut, that's when you get into trouble.**

Years ago, I was contacted by a prospect who was taking a serious look at our company and told me she'd done a lot of research and wanted to explore working with me. When I first talked to her, she told me she'd heard of me through an informational call I recorded about our company after seeing it posted on my wall. When I asked her if she was talking to anyone else working with our company, she said No. Over the next few conversations, it came out that she had been talking to another builder, but reported that she didn't gel with her personality. I followed my own rule and told her to loop back to the other builder to let her know she wouldn't be pursuing a business relationship with her. This prospect came back and reported she did so, and we continued our conversation.

Then—and this is where I should've politely and respectfully told her to join someone else's team and wished her well—she told me she had been talking with another biz owner, but she couldn't possibly join her because she had "issues" with the other biz owner's significant other.

I'll admit it, she tugged at my heart with her story of what was going on in her family, how hard she was willing to work, how coachable she'd be, how much she needed this opportunity, that the others weren't a good fit for her at all, and that I was the only one she would grow a business with in our company. But here's the thing. If I had been thinking with my business brain and tuned into the slightly icky gnawing in my gut, instead of thinking that I could be the one to "save" this woman, what happened next wouldn't have happened.

It turned out that the two other builders she had talked to were on my team. She hadn't fully made it clear to them why she didn't want to join their teams. And she didn't tell me that she had heard about my info call through one of them. My team member, like many on our team, used the call to help close her prospects and grow her team. But I was the one who enrolled her. Yuck.

What ensued was an absolute shitstorm. Their uplines, valued colleagues and friends, were royally pissed at me. My team members lost trust and respect in me because I enrolled a woman who, it turns out, was talking with two other team members before she came to me.

Now, you could say that based on the facts I had been given, I followed the ethical rules of 1) asking the questions and 2) pushing back, so all was cool. But it wasn't. I'd failed them all by not doing enough fact-finding about the other people the prospect was talking to in order to find out the truth. It happened because I ignored that slightly icky feeling in my gut. This woman was talking to too many people to truly be available, and my gut picked up on it. Even if you could argue that she was available, she was undeniably flighty or squirrely and not a good prospect. I should've asked myself the question, "If she were a he, and those other builders were women he was dating, would you want to date him?" Worse yet, "If you were family with those other women, would you want to date him?" The answer would have been an unequivocal, "Hell to the No."

Turns out the woman wasn't consistent or coachable, and ended up doing nothing. She wasn't worth the time, energy, personal angst, or the anguish caused to others. Not only did it damage friendships I'd developed over the years, but it also turned out to be stupid business. Since then I have an iron-clad rule to never bring someone direct to me who has talked to others on our team first, no matter how unsuccessful my pushback. It's not worth it. I've learned that flighty, squirrelly people in your funnel grow flighty, squirrely businesses, which is to say they don't grow. Remember, everything duplicates. We all work so hard to build relationships with our teams based on trust and respect—even with those we don't know personally—and one stupid decision can chip a big old piece of that away. Even if this woman would've gone on to build huge, it wouldn't have been worth it.

Local Schmocal

It makes my blood boil whenever I hear that a business builder tells someone else's prospect that they'll only be successful if they join a local team. We all know that this you-must-join-with-someone-local line is bullshit, but it's happens a lot in every company. This happens because the person who originally introduced the prospect to the business lives in another town, another state, or even another country, and a local builder wants to steal that prospect. So here are a few things I have to say about that:

* If you believe that local is better, then your business should be confined to only your city, town, or surrounding area where you can meet face-to-face with your team members. But then you're not taking full advantage of our social commerce business that annihilates geographic limitations. And you're not a savvy turn-key entrepreneur in the digital age.

* This "strategy" is 100% against the supportive, collaborative culture that is one of the best parts of our profession. I've fallen completely in love with the encouragement and abundance pouring out of, not just our team, but also from builders across our whole company and even among leaders of other companies. I can't imagine going back to the cutthroat days of law or PR. But this "strategy" threatens this Eden, and it pisses me off.

* To pull someone away from a long-distance sponsor to enroll locally, or to create the fear that they won't be ac-

cepted or supported, is against our company's Code of Ethics, and is likely against your company's also. I guarantee that if you pull that crap, it will bite you in the butt when you're trying to grow from afar. Karma, baby.

Follow meeting and event etiquette.

We all attend events – whether they're business presentations, product-centric events, or others. At these events, remember you're surrounded by people, and you can assume that one or more of those people can hear everything that comes out of your mouth. So here's the Golden Rule for events. Before something comes out of your mouth, ask yourself if you'd like one of *your* prospects or team members to hear it.

> **Before something comes out of your mouth, ask yourself if you'd like one of your prospects or team members to hear it.**

I've personally heard builders at events complaining about guests canceling, customers quitting their auto-ship, or other negative statements. Do you think your prospects would be super-psyched to join you in business if they heard one of your colleagues say these things? Golden rule, people.

Then there's the Local Schmocal thing rearing its ugly head with events. In your company, like ours, builders often send prospects to events in other markets. Those people are supposed to feel welcomed and embraced, and made to feel like they'd be part of a local community even if their upline lives somewhere else. But we hear about poaching at meetings when the upline isn't there. It's just, what's the word, disgusting. There are enough people in the world who could be your customers and business partners that you don't have to prey on others' hard work, don't ya think? Karma, people.

Don't make shit up.

When you talk about your business and your products or services, be real about what's real. What it takes to build this. That it's not get rich quick. Don't embellish your stats or your company's stats. Don't doctor before and after pictures, or, for the love of God, steal another company's pictures. If you don't have all the facts about a person's success story or a product's efficacy, share what you do know and only what you know. You'll be much more helpful to your prospects if you tell them you need to find the information that they're looking for, than if you make shit up.

Don't assume that since a colleague posted something, that it's true. I mean, nothing false is ever put out on social media, right? So don't blindly post something just because someone else did. Stop and do a gut check, and a common sense check. If something doesn't seem right, investigate, or just go with one of the gazillion other fab things you can be posting, sharing, tweeting, or pinning. So when in doubt, check with your company's compliance or marketing department.

Don't post an implied celebrity endorsement of your business or products, unless that famous person has a contract with your company, or is your personal customer or business partner, and you have permission to use them in your marketing. (Or you know they're one of your colleague's customers or biz partners.) I giggle at all the clever, yet ridiculous, images out there that suggest Oprah or Ryan Gosling or Bill Gates is applauding our products or our business. If you do this, you open yourself and your company up to legal action from the celebrity. Aren't you glad I went to law school?

Even if you've done some of these things, I must share with you what John and I tell our kids when they do something that's not representative of their best selves. Just because you did that mean, underhanded, bullshit thing (and yes, we do cuss in front of our kids), you're not a bad **person**. You just had bad **behavior**. But now that you know the difference, you'll make better choices in the future. Every mistake is an opportunity to learn and grow. Every day there are wonderful opportunities to make good decisions that help people build other people up, and make you and your business stronger.

If you ever have a question, here's what to do. Kids have an unadulterated sense of right and wrong, so find a child between the ages of five and 13, whether it's your son, daughter, grandchild, niece, nephew, or neighbor kid, and explain the situation and what you plan on doing. No editorializing. No spin. No excuse-making. Just the facts. See if it passes their bullshit meter. If you find yourself wanting to editorialize, spin, or make an excuse, you know it's not passing yours.

Do what's right or karma will get you. Make good decisions. Now you know better.

CHAPTER 13

Your Time Is Worth $962 an Hour

In the next chapter I'm going to tell you that you've got to take care of yourself while you're building your empire. It may require you to add some things to your life. And that's going to piss you off. So first I'm going to tell you how to find more time in your day, your week and your month, so you can use that extra time to do the self-care necessary to be the CEO of your business and your life. I'm going to help you be more efficient.

Time is our most valuable resource.

Before we can have a compelling conversation about efficiency, you've got to understand how much your time is actually worth. First, you need to decide on two numbers:

1) How much do you ultimately want to earn annually from your business? Don't limit yourself to what you want to be bringing in next month or next year. I'm talking the big number. What do you want this business to grow into?

2) How many hours a week do you want to work? I'm not talking about what you think you **have** to work. You need to be honest about how many hours you **want** to work every week on your business.

Once I went to our company's first convention and started to understand what I had actually landed in, I started to think about my numbers. I wanted to earn one million a year and work 20 hours a week. I was dreaming big. Back then our company was so young, that we didn't have the success proof points we have now. We didn't have a Lexus program or a seven-figure earner, let alone a five-million-dollar earner. But I figured, what the hell, I'm going to shoot for the stars.

Since I'd always worked in professions ruled by the billable hour, I wanted to figure out what my time was worth. At the beginning of all our businesses, we're working a lot of hours for the promise of a big return. But I didn't want to focus on the depressing reality of what I was earning then for every hour of work I put in. Instead, I wanted to know what my time was worth—my billable hour if you will—based on what I wanted to earn.

Here are my calculations from back then:

20 hours per week x 52 weeks = 1040 hours per year
$1 million / 1040 hours per year = $962 per hour

Every hour of my time was worth $962! That blew my billable rate as a lawyer or PR consultant out of the water. Do you think that had an impact on how I spent my time? You better believe it did!

As my goals have changed—how much I want to earn and how much I want to work our business—I've consistently recalculated, so I'm crystal clear on my time's hourly worth. It helps me continue to refine where I spend my time and how efficient I am. As I write this, every hour of my time, based on my current goals of philanthropy, is worth $3846. Do you think this motivates me to keep working on greater efficiencies and not wasting time? You better believe it does.

Before we continue, stop and figure out your numbers.

Get in Action

Really think about what you want this business to create for you and your family. Then use those numbers to come up with your time's hourly worth. When you've got it, write it down below.

_____ hours per week X 52 weeks = _____ hours per year

(annual income) / _____ hours per year = $_____ per hour

Every hour of my time is worth $_____.

I hope you're thinking, "Wow, I'm the shit." Because you are. Or shit in the making. Either way, let's get you smarter about how you're spending your time.

After everything I've gone through and learned in the last several years as a mom, entrepreneur, and a very active human, I could write an entire book on how to better manage your time in your business and your life to really LiveFullOut. Hey, if you really like this book, maybe I will. But I want to give you the Cliff's Notes® version of some simple ways to find more time.

Manage your work schedule.

You may have already heard that to build a successful network marketing business, you must set your Hours of Operation—when you'll work your business every day and every week. For the first five years, I even trained on it. But I could never quite get them to work or get anyone else to stick to them. Why? Because Hours of Operation are total bullshit.

Since I started my business, I haven't had two weeks in a row that looked the same. Kids get sick. The water heater floods the house. A rush project in your day job gets dumped in your lap. Every week is different and even tomorrow may not look like what you planned. Am I right? So forget rigid Hours of Operation.

Instead, let me give you the simple system I use to ensure you'll show up in some form or fashion every single day for your business, despite everything else on your plate.

First, put everything you have to do in your life in one place. Whether it's a physical old-school calendar or an online one, everything needs to go in there. This includes your schedule and to-do's for your day job, your network marketing business, personal appointments, family responsibilities, work outs, social events, etc. If you're not religiously calendaring all of this stuff, get in the habit of doing so right now. The lives of CEOs of growing empires work because they schedule their lives.

> The lives of CEOs of growing empires work because they schedule their lives.

Second, instead of trying to establish Hours of Operation and sticking to them, here's what you're going to do. Every Sunday night sit down for 15 minutes with your calendar and map out the coming week. Look at everything you must do that's already in there; the things that are non-negotiable and non-moveable.

Third, identify pockets of time that you'll devote to your own prospecting. Remember, if you don't pay yourself first, your business won't grow. This time is sacred and is not to be used for anything else. Next, mark off when you'll be available for three-way calls and short coaching calls with your team. Finally, get your 5-3-2 list ready for Monday (the five new people you're going to reach out to, the three people you're going to reach back to and the two team members you'll touch base with).

What many builders, who are also wives and/or moms, find (me included), is that it's impossible to have a handle on our calendars and a juggling system that's a well-oiled machine without coordinating with our spouses. That's why years ago John and I started doing what we call weekly "traffic meetings" to coordinate each other's schedules and juggle responsibilities. We like to do them on Sunday evenings before he and I solidify our personal calendars. It's 15 minutes that has reduced stress, miscommunication, and frustrations, and made us more of a team. And it's helped us make sure the kids are picked up at their activities. I swear we only forgot Bebe once at dance. She still uses it to guilt us though.

Then, every day of the week before you shut down, take five minutes and look at the next day's schedule. You'll be able to do more juggling if necessary, get really clear about what the next day will hold, and gather your 5-3-2 list.

Fifteen minutes on Sunday night and five minutes every evening. Commit to this system for a month, and I promise you, you'll feel like you're proactively running your business instead reacting to it.

Your Stop Doing List

If you're finding it hard to find time for personal prospecting, then you're doing too much of something else. In the business bible *Good to Great*, Jim Collins argues that your "Stop Doing List" is just as important, and for many of us **more important** than our "To Do List." I encourage you to write down everything you do over the course of a week in your business, and how long you spend on it. And I mean everything. Be accurate and honest because that's the only way to reach your goals.

> **If you're finding it hard to find time for personal prospecting, then you're doing too much of something else.**

As a business builder grows an organization that will start to take on a life of its own, I strongly believe she should spend at least 85 to 95% of her time on personal prospecting, training newbies who are coachable and responsive, and doing three-way calls for her team. Those are the core activities required to build this business. Everything I've learned about this profession proves that to build something substantial, you really need to consistently devote 10-15 hours a week. So if you're not able to devote at least eight-and-a-half hours a week to the essential income-producing activities of prospecting, training newbies, and doing three-way calls, then you need to cut out some other things you're doing.

How long are you spending chit-chatting with team members, when instead you should be having very short, purposeful coaching calls where you talk about their three current business challenges? How much time do you spend rehashing the same concepts with your business partners, thinking that if you just explain the importance of consistent outreach one more time, she'll start to pick up the phone after six months of doing nothing? It may be more comfortable to have these conversations than the ones you need to be having with potential business partners and customers. But these time-suckers aren't going to grow your biz.

How much time are you spending trolling Facebook and thinking that you're doing IPA? Set a timer on your phone for five minutes. Pop on and make the post you need to make, comment on five people's posts so you have more visibility in their news feeds, give two team members a shout out, and get off. When the five-minute alarm goes off, you're done.

At the end of writing down every bit of business activity you're doing (or think you're doing) for a week, you'll have a good idea of what's not serving you. Stop doing them so you can spend your valuable and precious time focused on things that will actually grow your income.

Coaching calls must have a purpose.

Coaching sessions can be a real time-suck if you and your builder don't come to the call with a clear idea of what will be covered. After a team member has completed their first 30 days, which marks the end of the "newbie" phase, I offer weekly or twice monthly, 15-minute POWERShots (aptly named for our Powered By You Team) to address specific, pre-determined topics.

All team members have to complete a coaching questionnaire and return it to me several hours before the call. It includes the following questions designed to understand how actively she's working her business, where she's spending her time, and what challenges we need to discuss:

* How many new people did you reach out to in the last week?
* How many three-way calls did you bring to your upline in the last week?
* How many three-way calls were brought to you in the last week?
* Did you have the level of activity you wanted? If not, please explain why.

Then I have them list the three topics they want to discuss during our call.

This system not only makes for productive and efficient calls, but it also requires the builder to reflect on her personal activity. It's made it much easier for me to diagnose issues and help team members refine and fix. If a builder is a no-show without notice and there's no emergency, we table the sessions until she's ready to treat this like a business and respect my time. And when a team member doesn't reach out to at least 15 new people a week for more than two sessions, we put the coaching on hold until she's ready to commit the time to talk to enough folks to grow. Am I a hard ass on this? Yes I am. But I know what my time is worth and someone has to be all in to get my time. If they're not all in, I know our company and general team training and resources provide more than enough for them to meet their goals. I hope you'll understand the virtues of being a hard ass too.

> I know what my time is worth and someone has to be all in to get my time.

Work with your body, not against it.

Each of us has a unique physiology that dictates when we have the most energy. It's important we recognize our biorhythms and work with them, not against them. For example, I'm not an early morning person. It usually takes me until 8:30 to be engaged and engaging. And from 4:30 to 5:30 p.m., I'm worthless for anything that requires creativity or focused discipline. Instead of trying to fight that, I work with it.

That's why I never do my own prospecting or schedule three-way calls during those times. Instead, I use my lower energy times to get things done that don't require me to be compelling or inspiring. I'm a total fireball from 10 a.m. to 2:30 p.m., and then again from 8 p.m. to 9 p.m. You want to be in my energy field during those times, trust me. So it's my prime prospecting time.

I encourage you to look at when you're setting aside time for prospecting, and make sure it's not when you're in your natural valleys, instead of at your peak.

The personal touch doesn't have to be in person.

Don't do anything in person that you can do over the phone or via FaceTime. I used to think that if I enrolled a new business partner who lived locally, I should do the first training in person.

What I found over time is that, regardless of where they lived, there was no correlation between those I had trained one-on-one in person and those I had trained over the phone. The ones I trained in person who weren't self-motivated, hungry, and coachable did jack, while someone three time zones away who trained over the phone had two business partners in her first two weeks. Training over the phone saves everyone driving time, and shows your new business partner that she can train team members in other cities and countries, use her time efficiently, and not believe in any preconceived geographic limitations.

I've also seen many business builders slow down their growth by thinking they have to meet with every local prospect. I quickly learned that it is important to qualify how interested a person is in learning more about my business and my products *before* considering whether or not we should meet in person. Initial conversations about the business should be brief—ten to 20 minutes tops—and it's a much more efficient use of everyone's valuable time to do it over the phone. If your prospect wants to discuss things further in person after that, I recommend including a three-way call in that face-to-face meeting, or meeting after the three-way call if you're unable to close her then.

You're busy. The people you're talking to are busy. So show your prospects how simple this business is to fit into their already crazy, full lives, and how there aren't geographic limitations to how much and where they can grow.

Don't get distracted.

We live in an age when distractions are bombarding us all the time. Alerts, notifications, texts, tags. Just watch a teenager try and do homework, and you'll see how technology, with all its virtues, has made it very difficult to focus on a task from start to completion. Then compound all that with the distractions that come from working at home—the dog, the laundry, workmen, kids and the refrigerator. If you don't learn to be disciplined about all of it, it can eat up the time you have to build your business.

A few tips:

* Check your email you use for your business only three times a day. Whatever it is, it can wait for a few hours. Use texting for more urgent matters, and ask your team to do the same. If something doesn't need attention in the next hour, it's not urgent.

* Check Facebook or Instagram no more than three times a day. Unless you're doing some type of social media campaign that requires you to respond in real time, you're not going to miss anything critical in a few hours. When you do get on social media set a timer on your phone for five or ten minutes. When it goes off, you get off, and get back to the other crucial aspects of your business.

* When it's time to do your personal prospecting, close all programs and apps that aren't required for your call. That way you can focus on the call you're making, and immediately go to the next call without getting distracted.

* Turn off notifications. When I'm not actively on email or social media, I don't want to be distracted by notifications. I know myself, and the temptation is just too great for me to take a look. So I have to turn off all notifications.

Multiply your time.

I'm not talking about multi-tasking. Multi-tasking, which has become a bit of a badge of honor, is when we do two or more things at the same time. Research shows that multi-tasking isn't nearly as efficient as we all like to believe, and it can even be harmful to our health. Even though we like to think of ourselves as Wonder Woman, our brains actually have a finite amount of attention and productivity. If you're doing two activities at once, unless one of them is automatic, like folding laundry or walking, then you're never fully "in the zone" for either one of them. And if you're trying to juggle three or more things at once, forget about it. You won't be doing any of them with excellence.

I know that multi-tasking heightens my stress, and elevates feelings of anxiety from trying to cram too much in at one time.

But a 2013 Stanford study shows that combining activities can help us achieve our goals without maxing ourselves out. Using "multipliers" is about doing one thing that satisfies multiple goals, instead of doing multiple activities at once. [Bixler Clausen, L. (November 18, 2013). 'Multipliers' are key to rethinking time. Retrieved from http://gender.stanford.edu/news/2013/multipliers-are-key-rethinking-time#sthash.DZhxBZYM.dpuf]

For me, I like to read and respond to emails and Facebook messages when I'm sitting with our kids during homework time. They're happy that I'm there, I get

> Combining activities can help us achieve our goals without maxing ourselves out.

to oversee what they're doing and answer questions, and my inbox gets cleaned out. I listen to training calls while doing cardio. I do three-way calls when doing everything from cooking, to putting away laundry (there's that damn laundry again; why can't our kids wear something twice!), to driving. Please note that I am not suggesting that you conduct business activity while operating heavy machinery like a car. However, once I got very good at fielding three-way calls, I found driving time to be a valuable source for doing IPA.

Get in Action

Think about the different ways you could put this into practice. Come up with at least three multipliers you could start implementing.

It's also incredibly helpful to group like activities together. According to many studies, moving back and forth between several tasks probably takes us longer to finish than it would to finish each one separately. So put your uninterrupted focus on each task that requires a specific mindset, and once you get in a groove, stay there until you're finished. This is why I schedule three-way calls back-to-back, coaching calls back-to-back, answer emails all at once, and dedicate chunks of time to personal prospecting.

Are you clustering similar activities together on your schedule? If not, I challenge you to get in the habit of doing so, so you can avoid the little time suckers that come every time you have to switch back and forth between tasks. Not only will you be more efficient, but you'll also feel less taxed, stretched, and frantic.

> Are you clustering similar activities together on your schedule? If not, I challenge you to get in the habit of doing so.

Ok, I found you some more time. So let's turn the page and talk about how you can take care of yourself. Because you can't build a huge organization if you don't take care of the most important person in it—YOU.

CHAPTER 14

Taking Care of You
Along the Way

One of the most valuable gifts of this business is that it can give freedom to those of us with the guts and grit to build it. The freedom to work where we want, when we want, with whom we want. The freedom to earn as much as we want. The freedom to have our cake and eat it too.

But I've learned the hard way that if you're not taking care of yourself along the way, not only will you not build as fast, but you also won't be as healthy, happy, and fulfilled when you reach your goals.

I know from personal experience. By the time I retired John from clinical practice at the two-and-a-half-year mark, I was a wreck. I was exhausted; I never felt fully present; I was bitchy; I was carrying around ten extra pounds from stress eating; and I wasn't as effective as I wanted to be in any part of my life.

I had to make changes. I had to take care of myself if I wanted this to grow as big as it could, and if I wanted to be a healthy person, a good mom, a good wife and a good human. I really wanted to be able to enjoy this incredible thing that was happening to me, our family, and our team.

I wanted it all. Physical, spiritual, and emotional health. Meaningful relationships. A successful business. Fun and spontaneity. I had the successful business part, but if I was going to get the other stuff, I had to learn how to take better care of myself and live in better balance.

Don't get me wrong—I'd long ago abandoned the myth that it's possible for anyone to have it all, at the same time. For working moms at least, I just don't think it's possible to have absolute balance every day. It can still be pretty damn hard for me to have it every *week*. But a life that *overall* has it all was my goal. Once we got John free from his practice, I started making it a priority to take better care of me, which I knew in turn would help me take better care of my family, my relationships, and my business.

This required me to work on my mind, my body, and my spirit. It also forced me to put in a little extra effort to put in some systems that I desperately needed to help me. My book about how to use this profession to build the life of your dreams would be incomplete if I didn't show you how to do it too. But it's going to require you to pour some time into you, just like I poured time into me, and still do.

You read that right. After chapters telling you all the work you need to put into building this sucker, I'm telling you to add something else to your effing plate. To make sure to spend more time, that you think you don't have, on taking care of yourself so that you can build a bigger and better business and be a more fulfilled human.

What? Add something else to your already full plate? Yes. That's exactly what I'm saying. If you just hurled an expletive at me, it's ok. I can take it. Six years ago, I probably would've thrown some pretty choice words at you, if you had told me the same thing.

But remember, we just found more time by getting you more efficient. Hey, I haven't steered you wrong yet, so please stay with me on this. I promise you that it's possible to build this sucker **and** take care of yourself at the same time! The best part is that when you also take care of yourself, you'll build bigger and have more fun along the way.

First, let's get clear about something. You can't do everything, so don't even try. It's hard to juggle it all: kicking ass professionally, being there for your kids (and being present while you're physically there), taking care of yourself, and having enough left over for your husband and your friends.

You certainly can't do everything you want to do while you're in start-up mode with your business. I consider all builders to be in start-up mode until their income is where they want it to be, and their team is duplicating month after month. It's not that you're a failure if you're not doing it all. You're simply human like the rest of us.

Learn to say No.

In this biz we celebrate No's. Hell, in this book I told you to go out and get 100 of them pronto. Then why, oh why, do we have such a hard time saying No? This little word is one of the most important words to learn to say in order to be a CEO of a growing business, while remaining a sane and happy human.

When I started my business I had to say No a lot. No, I can't take on extra clients just because you really want my expertise. No, I won't be able to teach Hebrew School this year. No, I can't head up the fundraiser for Montessori. It wasn't easy. I'm a woman after all, and somehow we've been programmed to believe we're supposed to do everything, and do it well. But No got a lot easier to say the more I said it. And a feeling of great relief came with saying No to the things that weren't serving my top priorities.

> No got a lot easier to say the more I said it. And a feeling of great relief came with saying No to the things that weren't serving my top priorities.

I also had to learn to say No to myself and those unrealistic expectations many of us set for ourselves. Do you ever find yourself rationalizing doing something you either don't want to do or don't have time to do, because you think you "should" do it? I'm not talking about flossing or paying taxes. I'm talking about things like over-committing to volunteer activities or throwing a huge neighborhood block party for Valentine's Day because it's our turn. I was should'ing all over the place, and I have a feeling you are too. The problem with should's is they don't support our priorities. If they did, they wouldn't be a "should." They'd be a "want to" or a "must."

> The problem with should's is they don't support our priorities.

Give me the name of a CEO of a seven-figure company who, when she was in start-up mode, cooked dinner every night, cleaned her own house every week, didn't have any child care help, and took on every volunteer opportunity offered to her. I'm serious, send me a message on Facebook with her name, and I'll send you a free gift. I'm pretty sure she doesn't exist. Just like Santa Claus and Wonder Woman aren't real. They might be great ideas for people living in a fantasy world, but not for folks in the real world. So come live in the real world with me. It's liberating.

I recognized pretty early on that if I was going to be one of those seven-figure CEOs that I aspired to be, I wouldn't be able to do everything either. I had to say No to some of the hats I was wearing in my life. One of those hats was Chef of the House. I've always loved cooking, and until I started my business, I was the cook. It was clear, however, that this chef needed to be chopped from the meals schedule, at least part of the time, so I could have more time to talk to people. Dinners became more often meal assembly (thank you, Costco!) or John started adding to his culinary repertoire beyond the infamous "pepper chicken" from early in our marriage. It was just chicken and pepper. I'm not kidding.

Another hat was "Frequent Volunteer." Before starting my business, I sat on non-profit boards, led steering committees, and taught religious school for little ones. I'm not a super hero, and operate on the same 24-hour day that everyone else does. So I recognized that I didn't have the time or energy to focus on my top priorities—my family, my new business, my health, and serving my PR clients—and still do all the volunteer activities I took on prior to becoming a turn-key entrepreneur. I knew I wasn't saying goodbye to that kind of service forever. In fact, once I had a lucrative business and the time freedom that comes with it, I was able to entertain requests for volunteering and choose the ones that spoke to my heart.

While you're building your business, say No to anything that isn't one of your top priorities. I promise you: if you say No more often now, you'll be able to say Yes more often later.

Say Yes to help.

When growing companies, all CEOs invest in the necessary human resources and infrastructure required to maximize productivity and revenue. In our profession, we need a fraction of the resources of traditional businesses, because we get to tap into the infrastructures of the companies we work with. But that doesn't mean we don't need help. Because the bigger your business gets, the more help you're going to need and want and be able to afford.

> The bigger your business gets, the more help you're going to need and want and be able to afford.

I remember an eye-opening conversation I had with my then-client, Nell Merlino. Nell was one of the founders of Take Our Daughters to Work Day (now the gender-neutral Take Our Kids to Work Day). At the time I was her

PR consultant, helping her promote her latest venture, Count Me In for Women's Economic Independence. I'm so proud of Nell. Count Me In has become the leading national not-for-profit provider of resources, business education, and community support for women entrepreneurs who, unlike those of us in network marketing, are doing the enormous lifting of building traditional businesses of their own from the ground up. I just love how our professional missions are now the same—to help women grow their own micro-enterprises into million-dollar successes.

Back before kids, I was driving Nell around Seattle on a press tour. She told me something that has stayed with me ever since. "You know the reason there aren't more women millionaires, Romi? Women don't delegate. They either don't know how to or they refuse to learn. And it's costing them dearly." I vowed right then, should I ever be in a position to grow my own business, I would delegate everything I could.

If you find yourself, like I did, unable to be a full-time, hands-on mom and still have the time and energy required to build your business, then I encourage you to get help with your kids. You are not a fraud if you have childcare. In fact, if you can't get all your IPA done while juggling your kids, childcare is an essential business expense.

I know some of you reading this are thinking, "Wait a minute, lady, I started this business so that I could build something around my kids." Well, me too. And you are. But I challenge you to introduce me to a CEO of a seven-figure business who didn't have at least part-time childcare while she was building her empire. Did Tori Burch miss a meeting with Neiman Marcus because she didn't have anyone to watch her kids? No, she did not. So why do you think that you're supposed to be able to build a huge business in the hour a day that your toddler naps?

As women we hold ourselves to such high standards, unreasonable standards really. You may hear stories in your company or in our profession of moms earning seven-figures who have no help with their kids, yet they home school,

> Why do you think that you're supposed to be able to build a huge business in the hour a day that your toddler naps?

bake all the school treats, and always have time for a work out and a bikini wax. If there are women out there who actually do all this, then I applaud them until my hands hurt. But I don't hold myself up to that standard, and neither should you. It's ok to need help.

As your business grows and you need to field three-way calls for your team while still keeping up your own personal activity, it's a necessary business expense and practice to ensure that you have a couple uninterrupted hours at least a few days a week to work on your business. If your kids' schedules don't allow for this, you must create it.

Even if your kids are in school, you still want to make sure you have a couple of babysitters available so that you're able to take advantage of business building opportunities that require you to go to an event at night or to a Saturday training. Or to get a workout in. Or a date night. This is not a sign of weakness or child neglect. It's smart business and smart living. Our sitters were instrumental in the growth of my business and the preservation of my sanity.

It also made no sense to me to spend my valuable time cleaning the house, when we could pay someone else $20 an hour to do it. I wasn't a big time earner when we hired our first cleaning lady. But I considered it a business expense. Remember, I'd already calculated that my time was worth $962 an hour. In fact, anything that could free up my time from doing the things someone else could do, like cleaning, laundry, and cooking, would allow me to spend more time on the business that could set us free. I treated this like a business and invested part of my earnings to create more time, so I could make us even more money. And it worked.

That's why I constantly tell our team now, "It's okay for your net take-home pay from your business to be lower today, so that your gross earnings can be bigger tomorrow." Consider the cost of house cleaners, prepared food, and child care as business expenses (even though the IRS won't let you deduct them), because these investments in your business will pay you back exponentially.

Say Yes to personal development.

I hope you've learned by now that your business will likely succeed or fail because of what's between your ears. That's why it's essential that you spend some time every day filling your brain with positive, insightful things to help you be a better you. If you haven't already done so, commit to daily personal development. It's a crucial part of growing your business and growing as a human.

The challenge I've found with my personal development is that when things get really crazy busy, it's the first thing that gets knocked off my plate. But it's the thing I need most, and do do. Whether it's five pages you read before collapsing at night, or a book on Audible that you have playing in your head while you're on a walk or doing dishes or putting on make-up (love those Multipliers). Just get it in every single day.

I find great wisdom and inspiration in books about our profession, business books, autobiographies, articles, and self-help books of all kinds. Make personal development part of your team culture. Talk about resources on training calls, in team emails, or Facebook group pages. Give your favorite books as recognition gifts and incentives. Do a book-of-the-month with your team, and at the end of the month come together, either in person or virtually, to discuss the biggest takeaways and how to apply them to your businesses and your lives.

Say Yes to exercise.

I don't care if it's a ten-minute walk twice a day while you're on a three-way call or listening to personal development, or a 25-minute DVD you pop in before everyone else in your house wakes up. You must make exercise a part of your weekly activities. It will clear your head, help you better manage stress, boost your immune system and your energy, and keep you from piling on the Freshman 15 that can be common in the first year or two of a new business. Trust me, the last thing you want to worry about before your Convention Gala or the fabulous incentive trip you earned, is whether you're going to fit into your dress or your bathing suit. Ain't nobody got time for that! Plus, when we're stronger physically, we're more confident. Which makes us more magnetic. Which helps us attract the people who will run with us. I do various forms of exercise six days a week to keep me strong, focused, energetic, and healthy. I know my commitment to moving my body has greatly contributed to my business. If you think you don't have time, I encourage you to reframe that thought. You can't afford **not** to exercise.

Say Yes to downtime.

When you're building a business of your own—any business, but certainly in network marketing—there's a pressure (real or self-imposed) to always be doing something in furtherance of your business. Add in a day job, a couple of kids, volunteering, and it's no wonder we feel like we have to be productive all the time. I'm here to tell you, that in a business where we must be magnetic and patient and resilient, downtime is essential.

Scientific research shows that the brain at rest is actually replenishing its reserves of attention, motivation, productivity, and creativity. Those are the very qualities that allow us to work, so making sure they're in ample supply is crucial to our personal and professional success. Research also shows that people who have regular downtime are more satisfied with their jobs and have improved work results. [Jabr, F. (2013). "Why Your Brain Needs More Downtime", Scientific American.]

> In a business where we must be magnetic and patient and resilient, downtime is essential.

You don't need to spend a ton of time doing this to see results. Research by organizational psychologist Almuth McDowall at Birkbeck University of London shows that what's important is not how much time you spend recharging your batteries, but that you spend your time doing something you want to do. Take a yoga class, carve out some quiet time to read, do some journaling while you sip a cup of tea. It's quality, not quantity, that counts.

I've seen many business partners—myself included—ignore our personal need for stillness, frivolity and fun, thinking if we're in constant motion, constant activity, it will make the difference. But if we don't put on our own oxygen mask first, how can we help anyone else? For me, my oxygen mask comes in 10-20 minutes of daily meditation, a weekly decadent nap, and a couple hours a week of indulgent TV (my faves are Scandal and Super Soul Sunday on OWN). When these things don't happen, I really feel it and so does everyone else in my house.

If you're working smart, increasing the efficiency of your business, you'll have time for downtime. You'll feel better and more in control of your schedule and your life. Your business will grow. It's not that you don't have time for downtime. Truly. It's that you're succumbing to time suckers, including should's, and you're spending what downtime you do have on things that you don't enjoy. So it's not replenishing you.

Downtime can't be work. A lot of people in our profession think they're having downtime when they're actually doing work, so it's not replenishing them. In our profession, scrolling through social media isn't downtime, because that's part of our work.

I totally get the constant pull of social media, especially Facebook. A lot of it is rooted in FOMO (fear of missing out). We're afraid we're going to miss a great post from a colleague that we can use to promote ourselves. Afraid we'll miss a message from a prospect who's in our funnel. Afraid we'll stop being relevant to our audience.

Then there's the constant checking that comes after we take the time to craft a post. How many Likes did I get? Are there any comments I can mine for leads? And on and on it goes.

> I totally get the constant pull of social media, especially Facebook. We're afraid we'll stop being relevant to our audience.

I love social media, am admittedly mildly addicted, and know it's been a huge part of the growth of my business. It's helped reach more people to promote our business and our products, and has been an indispensable part of our team communications. I've talked about how to discipline your use for business and that it can't take the place of the offline interactions and relationship-building that go into this business, so I won't beat that to death.

But when I coach the virtues of taking time for ourselves, there are invariably some who respond that they don't have the time to fit it in. This may be true, but first I ask them to monitor how much time they spend surfing the Internet or scrolling through Facebook. I give them the homework I'm now giving you.

Get in Action

Over the next seven days, write down every instance you find yourself with a little time on your hands and you start trolling social media. Since you're monitoring yourself, you'll probably be underreporting how much time you're actually spending. But the research might give you a clue.

Americans spend an average of two hours a day trolling our social media accounts (most of it on Facebook); and in our profession, it's likely more. [2013 Study, Ipsos Open Thinking Exchange] Because social media is part of our work, how can this possibly be relaxing downtime that recharges us and fills our souls? So stop using it as a downtime activity!

What do you love to do? What feeds your soul, clears your head, puts a smile on your face? If you've done all the other purging I've suggested in these pages, I know you can find the time to sprinkle them throughout your week.

Start your day the right way.

When we wake up, we've got to feed ourselves before we start feeding anyone else, including our business. And I'm not talking food.

When my business really started growing, I would wake up and immediately check my email, texts, and Facebook to see if I'd missed anything while I slept. This was exacerbated when we moved from the Mountain Time Zone to the Pacific. I figured if I could respond to a few emails before the kids got up and answer some questions on our team page, that I was in control of my day from the beginning. But I wasn't. It was the exact opposite. I was letting other people control my day from the beginning. No wonder I felt like I was playing catch-up all day long. I hadn't taken the time to check in with me.

The beautiful thing is that each of us gets to decide how our day starts. I vote that mine should start with gratitude, positivity, and inspiration.

First, if you use your cell phone as an alarm clock, stop it. Put that damn thing somewhere you won't see it when you wake up—until you're done starting your day your way. If you don't, the minute you reach to turn off your alarm, you'll be tempted to start checking email, texts and social media. From the minute you wake up, you'll be in reacting mode.

I like having a morning ritual because it sets the tone for my entire day. When I miss it, I really feel it. My morning ritual is that once I open my eyes, I think about one thing I'm grateful for. Then I mentally set my intention for the day. It's not a review of my to-do list, but how I want to approach the day. For example, this morning my intention was Peace. I knew I had a lot of things to tackle and some things that would disrupt my usual schedule. So I set the intention to stay peaceful throughout.

Think about what you can start doing every morning to capture a few minutes for yourself to set the tone for your day. Now do it for three weeks without exception. I promise you, it will rock your world.

Unplug.

This one was really hard for me in the first few years, but it's so necessary to have set times when we completely unplug from our work and technology—daily, weekly and for longer stretches every year. Research shows that unplugging leads to greater productivity and actually helps your team to develop their own skills and leadership.

> **Research shows that unplugging leads to greater productivity and actually helps your team to develop their own skills and leadership.**

A study by Harvard Business School professor Leslie Perlow challenged the notion that employees need to always be available to do a good job. Perlow's findings, outlined in a recent article in the *Harvard Business Review*, involved teams of consultants at Boston Consulting Group (BCG)—a company known for its hard-driving, ambitious, and career-focused workforce. [Perlow, L. & Porter, J. "Making Time Off Predictable—and Required". Harvard Business Review.] We're not employees, but her findings are applicable to turn-key entrepreneurs like us who build and lead teams.

One of her experiments involved a team working on a project for a new client, and everyone in the group was required to take one full day off a week. In a second experiment, which involved a team working on a post-merger restructuring project, she mandated that each consultant take one planned evening off a week, during which the employee could not work after 6 p.m., even to check email.

She found that participants who had regular downtime reported greater satisfaction with their jobs, increased likelihood that they could envision a long-term career at the firm, and better work/life balance compared with BCG employees not taking part in the experiments. Participants' work benefited. The experiments resulted in more open communication among team members, which sparked new efficiencies with how the team delivered projects. Additionally, Perlow found that since colleagues weren't available all the time, it forced co-workers to better understand others' jobs, gain new skills and problem solve.

Just like the subjects of Perlow's experiments, we all need to have time when we completely unplug. That means turning off our phones for a period every single day so that we can be fully present for something other than our work. I do this during the kids' homework time and dinnertime, so our kids know they have my undivided attention. Two nights a week, after the kids go to bed, I shut off my phone so John has my undivided attention. It's also important to unplug from work one day a week. I understand if you're working your business alongside a full-time job, it may seem impossible to take off an entire day and still get in the IPA you need. But I encourage you to spend your business building time on true IPA, and practice the efficiencies I've taught you. I'm willing to bet you're actually able to completely unplug one day a week and attack the other six with even more gusto and efficiency.

I'm also a big believer in unplugging from our businesses for a string of days once or twice a year. Even if we're routinely practicing downtime activities and unplugging regularly, human bodies and minds need vacations to avoid burnout and be able to bring our best selves to our business and personal lives the rest of the year. Besides, a vacation isn't a real vacation if you're working through it.

Plus, you're not the only one who needs you to take real vacations. Your team needs to see you do it. Everything duplicates, and you want them to duplicate a balance between work, their families, and self-care. Your kids need to see this as well. How can we possibly raise children whose heads aren't always in their devices, who know how to be fully present, and have actual conversations while looking other humans in the eye, if we're not modeling it for them? We can never ask our teams to do things we're not willing to do. The same applies to our kids. Let's teach our kids to work hard—in a focused and efficient way—and to also enjoy the rest of their lives.

Still not convinced you can unplug? Just try it for a month. If you're doing everything else you should be doing throughout your days, weeks, and year, then soul-soothing unplugging will actually improve your health, happiness, and bottom line.

Celebrate the little victories.

Get in the habit of rewarding yourself for the effort—the activity—not the outcome. We all do things that are little victories every day, but we sadly don't acknowledge them. Making calls to five new people. Reaching out to the scariest person on your chicken list. Having a frank conversation with your business partner about her goals and lack of activity to meet them, even though it was really uncomfortable. It's the little victories that lead to the big ones, and celebrating and rewarding ourselves for those successes along the way keeps us motivated to keep going toward the big hairy audacious goals. When you make acknowledging and celebrating little victories part of your team culture, it will make a big difference in the confidence level of your team members. If you're a parent, I encourage you to celebrate little victories—both in your efforts and your kids' too.

> **It's the little victories that lead to the big ones.**

Building a six- or seven-figure business is hard. It takes courage, discipline, grit, vision and a big set of cajones. Some days you're going to feel like you're failing miserably and that you'll never get where you want to be. But I'm living proof that you can, and you will. It takes time. So in addition to being kind to yourself, practice patience. That doesn't mean you should be complacent or not attack your business every day with commitment and excitement. But while you have complete control over what your personal IPA is, you have no control over your personal numbers game and when runners are going to join your team. I love what Warren Buffet said, "No matter how great the talents or efforts, some things just take time. You can't produce a baby in one month by getting nine women pregnant." Be patient. It will happen.

Be kind to yourself.

You're going to have days when everything goes to hell. Your best-laid plans for productivity, self-care, successful IPA will go out the window. You're going to botch prospecting calls. You're going to piss off one of your team members (trust me on this one). But when you do, cut yourself some slack. Show yourself some grace and kindness. All any of us can ever ask of ourselves is that at any given time we do our very best. And some days, your very best may be mediocre or pretty crappy. That's ok. You're a work in progress, just like the rest of us. Acknowledge it, learn from it, and move on.

Let's be really honest here. While you're slogging up the mountain toward your goals, and even after you've reached the summit like I have, you're not going to have it all, all the time. That's why you've got to

> You're going to have days when everything goes to hell. Show yourself some grace and kindness.

do everything possible to take care of you along the way.

But some days you do get it all at once. My having-it-all days look like this: a great workout, some seriously productive work, lunch and a mani with a dear friend, watching Bebe in her dance class, a "deep" conversation with Nate about his goals, bathing and cuddling our four-legged daughter, speaking in front of 450 people who want to dream bigger, a late-night

date with John and our BFFs to celebrate the latest Lexus earners on our team, then snuggling with John as we both drift off
to sleep. Your perfect day may look entirely different. Until you
build a large, self-sustaining business and are able to leave your
day job, they'll be rare. But they do happen. And when they do,
it's magical.

Don't get down that you don't seem to be able to have
it all and do it all. Building a big business requires sacrifice.
You have to prioritize your time. Taking care of you has to be
part of your priorities. Because YOU are your most important
team member.

CHAPTER 15

It's a Family Affair

It's impossible to build this business in a vacuum. You want your significant other to not only know about and understand your business, but to also be your biggest cheerleader. I want to help you involve your family in your business and traverse the landmines that can pop up. Even if you're not in a committed relationship or don't have kids, this is still important stuff to understand, because you will have team members who must learn how to involve their families in their businesses. While I know families come in all different shapes and sizes, for the rest of this chapter I'll use "husband" as the catch-all term for spouse, wife, serious boyfriend or girlfriend, and ball-and-chain.

Tell them WIIFT.

Your business will affect your husband and kids in ways that will be uncomfortable, inconvenient, threatening or annoying for them. Trust me, it's inevitable. But if they know not only WHY you're building your business, but also what's in it for them, it will make it easier for them to accept the new normal of you and your side biz.

This business is a big change for your husband, and you need to acknowledge that. No matter how busy you were before, you've added another thing to your plate that means less time for other things, including him. He may have to take on more family and household responsibilities. He may get less

> You want your significant other to not only know about and understand your business, but to also be your biggest cheerleader.

attention, including less sex. So it's imperative that he not only understand WHY you're building your business, but also what's in it for him.

If your husband has shouldered the responsibility of being the primary breadwinner and you want to bring in more money to pay for household expenses, then tell him that you're committed to taking some of the financial burden off of him to reduce his stress. If you want to build an escape from your day job, explain to him that you want to be able to leave your job so you have more joy and energy to give to him and your kids. If you want to build a bigger vacation fund and your husband loves to golf, explain that you want to be able to afford more luxurious vacations that will include time on the golf course for him. You get the idea.

Remember that what's in it for him must be something you know he actually wants. Just because you have stories of wives retiring their husbands, don't assume your man wants to be retired from his career unless he's told you so. If your husband loves what he does, he may actually resent you lumping him into that category. Instead, find reasons that he'll really like.

When he understands the benefits your business can provide for everyone, it's more likely to make for positive and productive discussions—like the weekly traffic meetings I suggested the two of you do in Chapter 13, and talking about hiring the help you need to better leverage your time (covered in the last chapter). It will also make it a no-brainer for him to share with his friends how your business is helping, or going to help, eliminate some of his pain, and how it could do that for them too if their wives got involved.

No matter what age your kids are—toddler to teenager—they'll be affected by your business. They may have to get used to you not being at their beck and call, or having to shut their pie holes while you're on the phone, or even missing their tenth birthday because of your company's national conference (Nate still brings that one up when he wants to guilt us big time). Help them understand WIIFT so they'll be more helpful, accommodating and flexible.

The younger your kids are, the more immediate gratification the WIIFT has to provide. If you're trying to work your way out of your day job, WIIFT could be that "I want to work really hard to build my business big enough so I don't have to go to my other job that makes Mommy crabby and not as much fun to be with. Would you like it if I were happier and laughed more?" What kid would say No to that? As your kids get older, WIIFT can be farther in the future. If you want to fill their college funds, explain that you're building this business so they have more choices about where they can go.

> No matter what age your kids are they'll be affected by your business. Help them understand WIIFT so they'll be more helpful, accommodating and flexible.

When I started my business and Nate was a preschooler, I explained that I had to work on my other business while he played quietly so that we could see each other and hug each other whenever we wanted instead of me going away to an office every day. As they got involved in sports and other activities and proclaimed their love for their martial arts or dance classes, I'd use every opportunity to remind them that I was working so hard at my business to pay for their activities. When I wasn't around to put the kids to bed every night because of events, or when I'd travel to grow other markets, I would talk to the kids about our family goals and how I was working to make them happen. Nate and Bebe were both born with wanderlust, so using vacation goals with them through the years has worked like a charm.

We've also come up with family WHYs through the years using a family goal board. You may already be coached to do personal goal boards with a collage of pictures that declare what you're building toward. This is a powerful exercise to do alone and with your teams, especially if you keep your goal board in a highly visible place. It's also a powerful exercise to do as a family. It teaches your kids a valuable practice they can use throughout their lives, and having a visible goal board to work toward makes it easier for everyone to make the adjustments and sacrifices required.

Recruit your husband.

I'm not suggesting you bring your husband into your business as a builder, although that may happen. I'm talking about making sure your guy has a basic understanding of your enterprise and involving him in the parts of your business that affect him. That's why the first three-way call you should do with your sponsor, even before your Dirt List calls, is one with your husband. You want him to be your biggest cheerleader, to use the products or services you now represent, and be a source of referrals for you. This call is a valuable opportunity to make sure your husband understands the business, address any concerns he has that weren't addressed while you were considering the business, and educate him on how helpful it will be if he helps you add to your prospect list over the next several weeks with people he knows.

> **The first three-way call you should do with your sponsor is one with your husband.**

I also encourage you to share information that you find exciting and compelling, not just when you first start your business, but throughout your career. Ask your hubby if it's ok if you share about your challenges, explaining that you're not asking him to fix anything (which is a man's knee-jerk reaction), but that you just need to vent and receive moral support. Also ask him if he'd like to hear about your team's big and little victories. It will help him be a part of your business and your vision.

Another important part of recruiting your husband is establishing routine meetings to talk about schedules, juggling, and how we can help each other do all the things we need to do. Remember, in the short run, your new business may add more to your husband's plate, and that may feel uncomfortable for him. These monthly business meetings—and I encourage you both to think of them as business meetings—may be really different for your marriage, but they're essential. Since life changes, and kids' schedules and day job demands are in flux, your monthly meetings will be able to accommodate the fluid nature of your lives.

Each of you should come to these meetings with your schedules. And have a candid conversation about what each of you can juggle to help one another. These meetings should cover not only the weekly ins and outs of running your family, but also brainstorming about bigger picture strategies on how to free up more time for both of you. For example, in one of these meetings, you may decide you're willing to trade fancier date nights with a babysitter for stay-at-home movie nights with take-out while the kids are playing at the neighbors, and that will allow you to afford a cleaning lady twice a month to free you both up from a lot of the house work. These meetings must happen when you can be uninterrupted by kids, phones, and other distractions. And they must be sacred—meaning you don't cancel them. They have to happen. Plus, if you have them while you're out to dinner, guess what, you're talking business, so it could be a tax deduction! (Disclaimer, I'm not a CPA so for advice on eligible deductions, please consult with your tax advisor.)

In addition to monthly meetings, weekly ten- to 15-minute traffic meetings will help you both get your ducks in a row for the week. These help to reduce surprises and frustrations that can come from not understanding each other's schedules or forgetting commitments.

John and I have been doing our monthly business and weekly traffic meetings for years. In addition to helping me grow faster and making our lives and family run more smoothly, they've led to a very important side benefit for our marriage. Even though this may be your business, and your husband has his profession, working together like this to juggle it all brings you closer and makes each of you feel a bigger part of each other's life and success. Even though John wasn't out there prospecting for me or leading trainings for the first four years of my business, he knows my successes were his too because he saw—and I constantly reminded him—that he had a big impact on what I was building.

Leverage your husband's network.

Just like you, your husband has a network. People in his network could end up being your business partner, customer, or connector to a big builder. Your guy is sitting on a potential goldmine and he needs to understand that. The more he taps into his network, the faster you can grow. While John was incredibly helpful to my business in other ways, he didn't tap into his network for the first few years. Now he readily admits that was a big mistake, kicking himself for not reaching out right away to help us grow even faster.

Ask your husband to sit down and make a list of all the people he knows who are influential, successful, know a lot of people, have magnetic personalities, are between jobs, or have wives. Just like you, your husband can't prejudge how he thinks they will or won't fit into your business. Like you, once he gets in the habit of thinking of people, he'll start thinking of others, even at the most random times. So encourage him to capture those names in his phone or a little notebook to add to his list. Get in the habit of asking your hubs to spend 15 minutes adding to his list. Pour him a glass of wine or a beer and give him some space to comb through his memory, Facebook friends, yearbooks, and phone.

> Your guy is sitting on a potential goldmine and he needs to understand that. The more he taps into his network, the faster you can grow.

Once he has a list, then the two of you need to figure out the best way to reach out to each of those people. There's no one-size-fits-all way to do this. A lot depends on your husband's relationship with the contact.

In frequent short meetings (John and I tack on an additional five to ten minutes to every traffic meeting), talk about the people on his list, working in groups of 10-20 at a time. There are people that your husband will likely feel most comfortable simply handing you the contact info. When you reach out to that person, you'd kick off the conversation by saying, for example, "John suggested I get in touch with you to pick your brain about my business since you're so well-connected in Boston." There are others who may need a quick warm-up before the hand-off, like a phone call or email from your husband that sounds something like, "My wife's business is expanding into Seattle, and I told her I thought you'd be a great resource since you're so well-networked there. I'd love to connect the two of you so she can tell you who she's looking for. Can I give her your phone number? When's the best time of day for her to reach you?"

Or maybe the wife of one of your husband's contacts should hear about your business. Your husband can call or email him saying, "Jack, my wife's business is really cooking. She just paid our mortgage/she's covering all the kids' activities/she's paying for the family vacay this year, and I think Judy should take a look. Who knows, she might want to make some serious money and have a lot of fun doing it. What's the best way to get them together—phone or email?"

Your husband doesn't need to know more than that. If he gets questions he can't answer, he simply should say, "My wife has all the info. Let's connect you two." You may even find, like I did with John, that your husband actually has fun reaching out to people, and may want to better understand how to talk about your story and your business. Many active husbands on our team got more involved this way. It's a win-win, helping them get to WIIFT faster.

How to handle a not-so-supportive hubby.

Maybe your hubby, like mine, saw what you saw in this opportunity and was fully supportive of you starting your business. I'm forever grateful that when I started my business, John recognized the best way he could help me was by sharing many of the roles men in our parents' generation simply wouldn't consider. A few nights a week he cooked. We split laundry and cleaning duties, and then when it became clear that our time was better spent working on our respective businesses and being there for our kids, we used part of my earnings to pay for weekly house cleaning. He did a couple bedtime routines solo so I could go to events or hit the phones. Even around his busy medical practice, building his own entrepreneurial venture, writing books, and trying to get sleep, he supported me in any way he could.

I wish the same support for all of you. But I know from many on our team that not every husband is supportive. Maybe your guy is even taking every possible chance to be, shall we say, less than supportive. I can't pretend to understand what that feels like, or how tough it must be to do the heavy lifting this business requires and not have your most important partner in your corner. I'd like to be able to guarantee that he'll come around, but I can't.

Just know that many husbands do come around. Our dear friend and business partner Jamie Petersen didn't have her husband Bret's full support when she first started. Bret didn't see this as a serious business. A hard-working financial advisor, he would get annoyed when he'd come home from a long day at work and Jamie would need to go out to a business event, leaving him with their two young kids. At first, he wasn't happy with the pace of growth given Jamie's time investment, and didn't see what was in it for him and his family in the long run. Instead he was focused on how he was being inconvenienced. But Jamie, whose previous career was in the stock market, knew the potential and knew what she had to do to create the financial vehicle she wanted for her family.

Once Bret started seeing serious money coming in and the growth trajectory, it got his attention. The formerly annoyed and inconvenienced husband became his wife's biggest cheerleader and a catalyst for husbands getting more involved in their entire team. Today they're enjoying a seven-figure business. While Bret maintains his own career that he loves, he also teaches husbands on their team how to help their wives grow faster and does business-building events. Now he does whatever it takes to be Jamie's

50-50 partner in their entire life, which now includes three adorable and very active kids.

Sometimes it takes even longer for husbands to come around. I remember comforting a sobbing business partner on an incentive trip after she had yet another anguishing phone call with her husband who was home with their toddler. Her husband complained every time she had to leave their daughter with him because of her business, and it was tearing her up. This was even after she had already reached huge success with her business and was able to retire from her career. She didn't let it derail her goals, and stayed committed to her vision of getting her family out of debt and leaving her job so she could be a stay-at-home mom. I'm so proud that my strong friend didn't let her husband's issues derail her goals as she built what's become a seven-figure business and set up a scholarship fund. Her husband did eventually support her, embracing the opportunities he had to build a stronger bond with his daughter, and accompany his wife at big company events and on luxury incentive trips.

Look, there's no guarantee that your now-cynical husband will see the light, start supporting you, and jump in and help you build your business. But know that many successful business builders started out without the full support of their spouse and ended up having them completely on board. It can take money coming in for a while for your husband to really see what's in it for him and for the family. Until that time comes, stay focused on your business, surround yourself with as many positive people as possible, and fill your head with personal development every day.

Make your kids part of your business.

I've always tried to find ways to make the kids feel included in this business. And that began by referring to it as "our business" or "the family business." When the kids were really little, I would give them a toy phone and computer so they could do their "work" while I did mine. This could be why some of Bebe's first words were "eye cream" and "peptides." I'd give them little jobs to help the family business, even if it wasn't all that helpful, just so they'd have more ownership of the success. This included emptying the trash can in my home office, organizing pens, shredding paper, and anything else that was fun for them and made them feel empowered and valued. As the kids have gotten older, their contributions have become more substantial. Just last week Nate and Bebe helped me pick out beautiful jewelry I'll award the top performers in a coaching series I'm doing for a part of our team.

This business provides a priceless opportunity to teach our kids that it's possible to work hard to get what you want, while also helping others get what they want. A huge part of that is introducing the kids to our team. I've always made sure they got to know our team through Facebook posts and sharing about our business partners' families and successes. They not only know when I'm working hard toward a goal, but they also know when our business partners are running to earn a Lexus, a promotion or a trip. This has led to our beloved month-end dance parties where we crank up the music and bust a move with every big announcement.

I've also involved the kids in team recognition, from drawing on the envelopes of cards and packages, to lots of videos picking winners in incentive drawings and sending congratulations for promotions or trips earned. Because it's important to build a team culture that feels like family, it's been just as important for the team to get to know Nate and Bebe.

In fact, at ten, Nate was the youngest guest ever on our weekly team call. He showed our team what his success selling poinsettias for the YMCA could teach them about setting goals and reaching them, and how to keep our business brilliantly simple. He shared gems like why he doesn't take "No" personally, "Why would I care? I'm not a poinsettia." I was one proud mama as the rave reviews came in from our peeps across the U.S. and Canada, crediting Nate with helping them have aha moments and big breakthroughs. Some moms even passed the call along to their Girl Scout daughters to get them ready for cookie season. Do you think it boosted Nate's self-confidence and increased the ownership he feels for our business? You bet.

This business has made me a better wife and mom. It's made John a better husband. It's made our marriage stronger. And our kids are growing up in a family that celebrates goal setting, hard work, commitment, teamwork and the success of others. Everything this profession has taught us has spilled into our parenting and into Nate and Bebe's evolving characters. It's one of the most unexpected and invaluable parts of this gig. I wish the same for you and your family.

> **Our kids are growing up in a family that celebrates goal setting, hard work, commitment, teamwork and the success of others.**

Chapter 16

#FUCKFEAR

You can read hundreds of phenomenal books on how to build your business, and I hope by now you think this is one of them. You can listen to as many training calls as you can find every week, although by now you know why I strongly discourage that. You can be the direct business partner of the biggest superstar in your company. You can even understand all the ins and outs of this simple, duplicable system. Even with ALL THAT, there is still one thing that will keep you from success.

Fear.

This little four-letter word can have the destructive power to annihilate all of your intentions. All the bullshit stories you're making up in your head? Fear is behind all of them.

Here's the bad news. We humans all have fear and there's no way to escape it. I'll never forget when John and I watched our then five-year-old daughter Bebe in her first dance recital. Her little confident self, along with her fellow dancers, pranced and strutted all over that stage. They didn't remember all the steps. They certainly didn't carry out flawless performances. But they danced their little hearts out, with unbridled enthusiasm. With pure joy. Without fear. Yes, they were very proud of the costumes they were wearing, but what really struck me is that they were naked little souls. They were how God intended them to be.

See, at their age, no one has told them yet that they're not naturally talented, or that they shouldn't try and dance because they'll never be one of the few to make it on Broadway. No one's told them they're not pretty enough. Or tall enough. Or thin enough. Or that dancing isn't a respectable endeavor. And they don't have a track record of other disappointments or failures to squash their confidence. They're just dancing to the music simply because one day they decided they wanted to dance.

Fast forward a couple years, and Bebe's passion has advanced to the competitive troupe. The reckless abandon has already been tempered by a system that ranks and judges, has winners and losers. Her rehearsals, both in the studio and in her bedroom, have a new observer: Self-Doubt. She wonders, "Am I good enough?" "Can I do this?" "What if I fail?"

This is what happens to all of us. We experience disappointments. And failures. And rankings. And non-supportive relationships. Life happens. We get cloaked in fear. We're covered in it, and over time it can become so thick and heavy that it keeps us from remembering our dreams. What we're capable of. Who we're meant to be. It gives birth to voices in our heads that become so loud that we can't hear the real us anymore.

> We get cloaked in fear and over time it can become so thick and heavy that it keeps us from remembering our dreams.

Is it any wonder that despite having all the training and tools we could possibly need, that so few actually build the businesses they're capable of building? It's because the fear has drowned out the WHY, the coaching, the dreams and the possibilities.

To prove this point, I recently asked a small accountability group of 30 business builders on our team to write down all their fears about their business, screen shot it, and post it on our group's Facebook page. Here is the list of everything they admitted:

* Fear of not saying the right thing
* Fear of looking or sounding stupid
* Fear I'm exuding too much confidence
* Fear I'm not confident enough
* Fear of not being taken seriously
* Fear of what people think of me
* Fear of what people think of this business
* Fear of annoying all my friends and family
* Fear of pestering people
* Fear of being "that person" that everyone wants to run from
* Fear that I don't have what it takes
* Fear of not having the right network
* Fear of exhausting my network
* Fear of running out of people to talk to
* Fear I won't meet new people
* Fear of keeping my funnel full
* Fear of keeping my funnel too full
* Fear of not finding the right people
* Fear of investing time in the wrong people
* Fear of rejection
* Fear of getting a "No"
* Fear of a "No" changing our relationship
* Fear of being judged
* Fear of disappointing others
* Fear of disappointing myself
* Fear of letting my kids down
* Fear of letting my husband down
* Fear of letting myself down
* Fear of proving my critics right
* Fear of not proving my critics wrong
* Fear of stressing myself out

* Fear of putting too much pressure on myself
* Fear of not going fast enough
* Fear I've gone too fast and will hit a wall
* Fear of really applying myself and failing
* Fear of hitting a plateau and not moving past it
* Fear of not finding business partners
* Fear of not being able to train new business partners
* Fear of not growing a team
* Fear of not being able to lead a team
* Fear of not doing enough for my team
* Fear of not finding "runners"
* Fear of finding runners who will go way faster than me
* Fear of not finding people who see what I see
* Fear of the time I've sacrificed and it not being worth it
* Fear of not balancing team support with growing my personal business
* Fear of never being able to balance my business with the rest of my life
* Fear of my business getting too big to balance
* Fear of not making enough money
* Fear of making a lot of money and losing it
* Fear of success
* Fear of failure
* Fear of my team failing
* Fear of not sustaining success once I get there
* Fear of being good but not great
* Fear of not being efficient enough to grow big
* Fear of having to choose between my current career and this company
* Fear of going all in and then it gets taken away or collapses
* Fear of saturation

* Fear that my network will join someone else
* Fear of not being enough for everyone
* Fear of not being a good leader for my team
* Fear of not being as good at mentoring as my mentor
* Fear of not being able to bring three-ways
* Fear of the unknown
* Fear of never ever being able to retire because I was a chicken shit or too tired or too distracted
* Fear of letting "I can't" win over "I can"

Since I'm inherently "a fixer" and a lawyer by training, my first inclination was to argue the fallacy of all these fears. Surely if I could point out why each and every one of these fears can't survive an intellectual analysis, then they could move past them and on to unfettered IPA and great success. At the very least I could point out how comical this cluster is, showing many of these fears are chicken-and-egg arguments (if I don't try I can't fail), or in many cases, arguing both sides of the debate. If I could just help these team members better understand their fears perhaps they could quiet the negative voices in their heads. Maybe if they really understood the realities behind their fears, it would be easier to muster courage, and that courage might be more powerful than what is holding them back.

But I can't fix their fears or anyone else's, and I sure as hell can't argue them away. Fear isn't intellectual, pragmatic, or rational. Fear is emotional. As a #girlcrush of mine, Elizabeth Gilbert wrote in her epic book *Big Magic*, fear will always show up when we strive for great things and take risks because "fear *hates* uncertain outcome…This is all totally natural and human." It will always show up, and she thankfully adds, "It's absolutely nothing to be ashamed of."

Courage is routinely required to build our business. Since fear will always show up when we're embarking on the unknown and about to create something new and possibly fabulous and life-changing, fear and courage are not an either/or proposition. And it's not just Liz Gilbert who knows this. Nelson Mandela agrees. He said, "I learned that courage was not the absence of fear, but the triumph over it. The brave man (*or woman*) is not the one who doesn't feel afraid, but who conquers that fear." In other words, the brave act *in spite of* fear.

So here's the great news about fear: It's not our job to argue with it, or fix it, or escape it. **It's our job to act in spite of it.**

Yet in order to repeatedly act in spite of fear, our desire to go after our dreams has to be more powerful than the fear that's holding us back. So that, like Bebe, we dance because we have to.

Steven Pressfield, author of *The War of Art*, agrees that fear is actually a sign that we must do it. "The more scared we are of a work or calling, the more sure we can be that we have to do it," he writes. "The more fear we feel about a specific enterprise, the more certain we can be that that enterprise is important to us and the growth of our soul."

I've had fears my whole adult life. When I acted in spite of my fears it was because my desire to grow, stretch, dream and achieve was far greater than my fears. The fears didn't disappear. I just said, "Fuck fear, I'm doing this." Was it scary to leave a career that didn't fit me (lawyer) and a city that didn't feel right (Dallas) to go find myself professionally and personally in New York without a job and a place to live? Absolutely. But I wanted so much more than my day-to-day life. I not only wanted to take a big bite out of The Big Apple, but I also wanted to devour more of my life.

Was I scared to start a side business in the direct selling channel after more than 12 years of successful, respected, award-winning public relations work? You bet. Major butterflies were swirling in my gut for all the reasons this venture scares you. But my dreams of the life I really wanted were so much bigger. I have a long history of taking a deep breath, trusting my gut and pushing through my fears to get to the really good stuff. #FuckFear.

> It's not our job to argue with fear, or fix it or escape it. It's our job to act in spite of it.

I think it's because my biggest fear of all eclipsed all the little ones. My favorite Maya Angelou quote sums it up perfectly: "There is no greater agony than bearing an untold story inside of you." What scares me more than anything is not living the life I was meant to live. Not touching the lives I was meant to touch. Not teaching our kids to go after their dreams and to live their truth.

You're going to have fears. We all will. But make the biggest, loudest ones revolve around this: fear of what you'll miss out on if you don't go after your dreams.

Do you have the guts to LiveFullOut? I most certainly know that you do.

SOME FINAL WORDS

These are really valuable nuggets I've learned that I just had to share with you, but couldn't figure out where else to put them. So here you go.

Even though one can work from home in yoga pants every day, one simply should not. Those suckers stretch, making it difficult to recognize how lax one has been in shutting one's pie hole. Then, when it comes time to don cut-off shorts with buttons or a bathing suit (cue blood-curdling scream), one realizes the false sense of security one has been enjoying since said yoga pants still fit, while none of one's non-stretchy clothes do. Do yourself a favor, and vow to only wear stretchy athletic wear when actually doing athletic endeavors—the athleisure trend be damned!—and to change into structured clothing immediately after said athletic endeavor. Shower optional.

As you get more and more successful in your company and even the entire profession, don't get caught up in your own press. Don't chase the accolades and the recognition. Don't try and be the best, fastest, top earner, or biggest cheese. Try to be the best *you* can be every single day, for you, your loved ones and your team. There may not be a company title for that, but there's a life title—Servant Leader.

Don't wear bangle bracelets when you present from the front of the room, whether it's five people in a living room, or 550 in a ballroom. They're loud and distracting.

Don't give it away. My mother always told me, "They'll never buy the cow if they can get the milk for free." Admittedly, she was referring to me and dating, but there's a valuable application to our business. Too often I see professionals touting how great their products or their business opportunity are, and then they offer free-this and rebate-that to reach goals or finally get that person they just know will be their next racehorse. Please remember that you're looking for people who see what you see and are willing to invest money to enjoy the benefits of your products or the possibilities of your business. If you're discounting the proposition more than an occasional enticement, you're diluting yourself and all you have to offer. You're worth it, and so are your products and business opportunity. Believe it and everyone else will.

When posing for pictures (and in this biz we post a lot of pictures), don't stand with your arms flat against your body. It makes even the smallest, most-toned arms look big. Gently bend your elbow. I read this valuable advice from Kim Kardashian somewhere, and she's right. About this one thing.

When one of your close friends or family members poo poo's your business, and there will be at least one, simply tell them that you don't expect them to buy your products or join your team. But you do expect their support and respect. "I know there's more out there for me," tell them, "and I'm glad I have the guts and grit to go for it. Aren't you glad I do too?" Then let them do what they're going do, because their stuff ain't about you. So welcome them with open arms when they end up needing your product or your service, or when they need to replace the income from the job or the husband they just lost.

If you're ever feeling guilty about not putting your kids to bed for a few nights this week because you're running toward a promotion or helping one of your team members qualify for a big incentive, you might be surprised by how much of an impact you're having on their thinking and their future. Our kids have always let me know in ways big and small how much our entrepreneurial venture, and all the hard work that goes with it, is impacting their outlook on life. They're seeing what's possible for them, the power of hard work and to never give up.

When I finished writing the first draft of this book, I shut my laptop and started screaming for John and the kids. Through uncontrollable tears I yelled, "I just wrote a book! I just wrote a book!" The kids collapsed with me on the stairs as John looked on with a big smile on his face.

"I'm sorry I've been working so hard, but I really wanted to do this. I needed to do this," I sobbed.

In between kisses and squeezes, Nate (who's ten going on 70) and Bebe (who's seven going on 15) told me how "awesome" and "fabulous" the accomplishment was and how proud of me they were.

"See what you can do, kids, when you believe in yourself and follow your dreams?" I asked rhetorically through some major tears.

"I knew you could do it," Nate said, as he looked at me with those impossibly huge chocolate eyes.

And I know YOU can too.

XO,

Romi

Acknowledgments

A book, like a successful network marketing business, doesn't happen because of one person. And all the wisdom I've tried to share didn't happen because of me. It's because of the countless gifts I've received from many people who have shaped how I think, what I know and who I am. If it weren't for all of the people I'm about to list, this book would not have been.

To my sister Connie, whose best friend Ilene had a friend Susie who needed a PR pro and hired me, and then told me about her side gig. That's how this all started. I have enormous gratitude to all of you for leading me to the professional love of my life.

I'm forever grateful to Dr. Katie Rodan and Dr. Kathy Fields, and their husbands Amnon Rodan and Dr. Garry Ryant, for taking a chance on this business model and entrusting their legacy to people like me. Thank you for deciding to build another global success story and inviting all of us to come along for the ride. You not only changed my skin, you changed my life.

To Nicole Cormany, thank you for being the first to go on this wild adventure with me, and then retire your Josh so you could be one of the trailblazing couples in our company. I've learned so much from working with you and have loved watching you turn your business and your Cormany & Co. culture into a beautiful reflection of you.

To my former boss and now my fellow bossbabe Bridget Cavanaugh, you've made this gig so much fun. You continually inspire me to raise my game and have been a collaboration partner any CEO would wish for. I've loved watching your Dreamatologists turn dreaming bigger into a profession. I'm overjoyed this gig brought you, your Arnie, John and me closer together, and I thank you for being my bullshit meter and one of my biggest cheerleaders.

To Kim Krause, I will be eternally grateful for our Atlanta Summit that led to a friendship rich with long talks and rigorous debates about business and life, much dancing, eating and great respect. Many of our most beautiful and hilarious moments in this business involve you and your incomparable Rick. You and your team are at the Core of our success, and I will forever celebrate our Gotcha Day.

To Dorrit Karl, I'm still giddy that you chose me to be your mentor and am so proud of your courage and grit to keep digging deeper. Your potential is even taller than your stunning frame, and I can't wait to see what you do next for yourself, your girls, your Scott and your team as you continue to design your BIGLife.

To my month-end Voxer partners in hilarity (and many other days too), Amy Byrd and Marissa McDonough, I simply don't know what I'd do without you. Thank you for keeping it real, keeping me laughing and elevating the art of the working mom.

To Linda Lackey Ray, you bedazzle the world and anyone lucky enough to know you. Jamie Petersen and Jen Griswold, you've redefined what it means to GiVe in our business, and I salute you and adore you. Uber-classy, super smart and wickedly funny Christy Nutter, it's so fun to learn with and from you. Laura Meijer, you made me think differently about just how fast a fast start can be, while raising quads in killer heels. Lisa Ross, I love how we just get each other, and how you always make me think with my head and my heart. All of you fill my Tank.

One of the greatest gifts this business has brought us is you, Amy and Nick Hofer. You, Grace and Hailey are family, and your love and encouragement to write this sucker kept me going.

To Betsy Swartz, Erica MacKinnon, Debra Whitson, Pamela Mulroy, Amy Kearney, Tracy Willard, Jennifer Weatherbee, Dayna Chmelka, Brenda Flores, Kris Vandersloot, Candace Berde, Tracy Cater, Nicole Hartnell, Cindy Rutherford, Caryn Smith, Tricia Schatz, Elizabeth Doyle, Christa Wagner, Nina Perez, Penny Lind, Karis Campbell, Wendy Martin, Debra Santosusso, Emma Evans, Kirsten Dawson, Melissa Callahan, and April Gadberry, thank you for believing in yourselves and in me, and for teaching me so much about what it means to be a servant leader. And Lauren Myers, thank you for reminding me what strength looks like.

To the PBYou 10Xers, your collaboration, insights, hilarity and scorn for all things #cooter makes me fall more in love with all of you and what I do. Always remember you were Born to Sparkle.

To the rest of our team, thank you for continuing to inspire me to be better and serve you better. Every day I am Powered By You.

To all the people who didn't join me in business, or did and then quit, you taught me just as much as the success stories, and I'm grateful.

To my dear friend Lori Bush, thank you for teaching me that our true power comes when we're unapologetically authentic, hold an unbreakable vision and dedicate our professional lives to building others up. And that it's ok to be a tough cookie with a gooey center who cries when we see others do great things. I owe a lot of my success to your passion for the limitless landscape that is community commerce and your tireless work for our company.

To Leslie Zann, thank you for choosing me. When you worked at our company, you could've chosen anyone to mentor. But you picked this rookie and gave me more confidence to step into my own powerful voice. I treasure your wisdom, wit, ethics and our friendship.

To Oran Arazi-Gamliel, for locking arms with me in the early days of my new career and for teaching me some of my most valuable lessons.

Meredith Tieszen, my Montana soul sista, thank you for everything I can't possibly write about. We'll always have RegimenGate.

To Richard Bliss Brooke, thank you for not only wearing the white hat, but also for embodying everything it stands for. And for gently and persistently reminding me to get out of my own way.

To Sonia Stringer, you helped me find my voice and my boundaries again, and maneuver around the landmines that come with success. You are as elegant as you are ethical, and I love your contagious commitment to empower women all over the world.

To Ianthe Andress, thank you for trying to keep me organized from afar. I love having your cheery Aussie self on the other end of the phone, and I thank you for always having my back. Linda Branson, you fill in all the spaces I leave (and there are many), and made it possible for me to have writing time without the wheels coming off the bus. You also make it possible for John and me to fly off to be badass biz builders, or just have some peace and quiet and get some. Many, many days I am Powered by Linda, and I couldn't LiveFullOut without you.

To Lyla Held, my fifth and sixth grade English and writing teacher, you helped me fall in love with writing and helped me believe I had something to say. To Bryce Nelson, my beloved journalism professor, you mourned when I told you I was going to law school. But I eventually found my calling, and it involves telling many important stories. I hope you're proud of me.

To Loren Robin, Kimmy Merrill Brooke, Margie Aliprandi, Pamela Barnum, Michelle Fraser, Aimee Crist, Jules Price, Janine Finney, Lory Muirhead, Karla Silver and Sarah Zolecki for proving that our profession offers a remarkably collaborative and supportive sisterhood that's not limited to our companies. I love standing shoulder-to-shoulder with you and putting good out into the world. And laughing. A lot.

To every boss I ever had, I'm sorry. I know I was probably a real pain in the ass. Turns out I'm meant to be my own boss. Please know that my entrepreneurial spirit that likely drove you crazy has done a lot of good for others.

To my mom, Dee Rudolph, you've always told me I could accomplish all the things that were never options for you. Thank you for cheering me on so loudly as I built my business and wrote my book. And for holding back on the Jewish guilt when my writing kept me from seeing you as often. Sort of.

To Newt Rudolph, my dear dad, I like to believe that you are seeing all of this, and I have a sneaking suspicion you have a hand in it. Although I only got you for 28 years, I still hear you every day.

Writing can be a lonely business. So to Sadie our labradoodle, I thank you for keeping me company and my feet warm. Now that this sucker is done, I promise to take you to the park more.

To my Partner-In-Everything, thank you for your tireless edits, for not rolling your eyes when I missed yet another deadline, for believing I could do this even when I didn't. And for always helping me stand in my truth. I love you, and I love designing this life with you.

About LiveFullOut

Through our LiveFullOut community, John and I are dedicated to helping you design the life you really want. Visit www.LifeFullOut.com to get to know us better and get access to tips, training and inspiration.

Bulk Discounts

If you believe this book can help your established business builders and your new team members talk their way to the lives they want, we want to help you get a copy in their hands. We're thrilled to offer a bulk discount program so that you can save when you gift a copy to the people who are already part of your team, to every person who joins your team, and when you use the books as incentive rewards.

For more information or to order visit
www.LiveFullOut.com/Get-the-Book/

* * * * *

If you enjoyed this book, we'd be honored if you'd
spend a few minutes writing a review on Amazon.

CPSIA information can be obtained
at www.ICGtesting.com
Printed in the USA
FSOW02n1012100117
29456FS